THE
TWO VIENNAS

SECOND
WORLD WAR
ORAL HISTORY

CHRISTINE P. TANNER

This work has been recorded, transcribed, edited, researched, written and published by Christine P. Tanner, Oral Historian.

The Author is very kindly donating all of the profits from the sale of this book to the British Red Cross

Published by
CPT Oral History, Wiltshire, UK.
cptoralhistory@gmail.com

ISBN: 978-0-9569776-1-8

www.cptoralhistory.blogspot.com

The Two Viennas – Second World War Oral History
This is a work of non-fiction in aid of the Red Cross.

Cover and book designed and typeset by
Matt Swann of Matt Swann Creative Limited
www.MSCdesigner.com

Printed by Hobbs the Printers Ltd, Totton, Southampton, Hampshire, UK.

Front cover photographs: Mr Edward Freestone, Mr Norman Drummond.
Mrs Erika (Jennova) Brooke, Mr John (Donnarumma) Richardson.
Dove and Olive branch image, courtesy of Catharine Trowbridge www.catsclips.com
Photograph opposite: Bust of Henry Dunant at British Red Cross HQ, London.

This book is dedicated to the memory of
Henry (Jean Henri) Dunant 1828–1910
Humanitarian and Philanthropist
The Founder of the International Red Cross
and Red Crescent Movement
Originator of the Geneva Conventions
First Nobel Peace Prize winner 1901

and

To all the many Red Cross Delegates in the field, mostly anonymous,
past and present who risked, and continue to risk, their lives
on the battlefields, inspecting prisons or assisting in natural disasters.

CONTENTS

INTRODUCTION

My Prologue is a brief personal history of the tragic life of Henry Dunant, the Founder of the International Red Cross and Red Crescent Movement. He was also the originator of the Geneva Conventions and first recipient of the Nobel Peace Prize in 1901. I apologise for any errors or omissions.

From 1863 to date, many millions of lives have been saved or endured less suffering because of the vision and philanthropy of Henry Dunant. It was also through him that the foundations of modern International Humanitarian Law were made.

The following three Sections of the book are based on recollections of the Second World War obtained using my life history interviews, general conversations and extensive research. The first two Sections demonstrate the importance of the Red Cross in relieving suffering during war and its aftermath. My third wartime story includes some recollections on the exploitation of Algeria's land for liquid gas, water purifying, and Felfela's marble quarries. As with Dunant, Algerian land, water and marble played a part in the life of my interviewee. These three Sections of oral history, which are complemented by over a hundred photographs, document life histories and experiences that would otherwise remain untold.

This work of non-fiction is in commemoration of the seventieth anniversary of the end of the Second World War.

Christine P. Tanner,
Oral Historian, 2015

The views expressed in this book are those of the Interviewees and, together with other content, are the result of four years' research by the Author. Neither the British Red Cross nor any other Red Cross or Red Crescent organisation is responsible for the text of this publication. The Author wishes to thank the British Red Cross for authorisation to display the Red Cross emblem within the old black and white photographs in this publication on pages 41 and 47.

Blue bold text in the three Sections denotes the edited recorded or spoken word.

Black regular text denotes the author's notes and research.

PROLOGUE
HENRY (JEAN HENRI) DUNANT 1828–1910
A BRIEF PERSONAL HISTORY

MILLIONS OF PEOPLE THROUGHOUT the world do not know the name of the person who founded the Red Cross and who was the Originator of the Geneva Conventions and the first Nobel Peace Prize winner in 1901.Through the legacy of his philanthropy and drive millions of lives have been saved, and continue to be saved or altered. My Prologue is a brief life history of this man – both laudable and tragic, although ultimately inspiring.

On 20 June 1827 Jean-Jacques Dunant (1789–1875), a successful Genevan merchant whose father was a city councillor, married Anne-Antoinette Colladon (1800–68), the daughter of the medical director of the Geneva Hospital and mayor of Avully in the Rhone Valley. The couple were from wealthy, influential, Calvinist and civic-minded families. Jean-Jacques was also a superintendent of an institution for orphans and a supervisor of prisons. His wife was involved with charitable work for the poor or sick.

In Geneva, on 8 May 1828, Anne-Antoinette gave birth to a son, Jean Henri Dunant, to be known as Henri. Thereafter, Jean-Jacques and Anne-Antoinette had four more children – Sophie-Anne (1829–86), Daniel (1831–1904), Marie (1833–1920), and Pierre Louis (1834–1918). These children grew up in a religious and altruistic environment at their home called La Monnaie in Petit Saconnex on the outskirts of Geneva, where they were surrounded by beautiful gardens with views of Lake Geneva and Mont Blanc. They often accompanied their parents in their voluntary work with orphaned children. They also visited the sick, or read to inmates in Geneva prison. Carefree days were spent in the homes and gardens of their grandparents, taking family carriage trips to the Jura, or travelling further afield to visit their great Uncle Daniel in Marseille with whom their father often conducted business. The children led an idyllic and tranquil life.

At the age of ten Henri Dunant attended the prestigious College de Geneve founded by Calvin. Henri rarely took part in organised games, preferring to read, which was his greatest pleasure. He chose to take his mid-day meals in the peaceful surroundings of his Aunt Sophie's home which was close to his school. He was greatly influenced by his immensely pious mother. He was also tutored by the local pastor's wife. These factors appeared to inhibit his natural maturity and slowed his independent development. By his teenage years Henri was 'earnest, believing and serving the Lord'. He was a child of the 'Reveil' – Evangelism – though with an enterprising, tireless zeal.

When Henri was eighteen he joined the Geneva Society for Almsgiving, and the following year, together with colleagues, he founded the 'Thursday Association', a bible study group which gave help to the poor and undertook prison visits and other social work. By 1851 he had become a member of the Christian Association of Geneva and a committee member of the Evangelical Alliance. He founded the Geneva chapter of the YMCA in 1852, also becoming a founder member of its international organisation in 1855 where he stood alone proposing 'internationalism and neutrality'. The seeds of philanthropy were within Henri but he was possessed with a missionary fervour and a dynamic enthusiasm which, at times, caused him to be hasty in his judgements.

Henri's parents decided that religion was not going to provide him with sufficient means of income. Consequently, he was apprenticed to the money-changing bank of Lullin and Sautter with whom, in 1849, at the age of twenty-one, he succeeded in acquiring employment. Four years later he was offered a position as cashier with La Compagnie Genevoise des Colonies Suisses de Setif, a firm which had connections to Lullin and Sautter which was devoted to the expansion of French colonialism in Algeria.

In his new job Henri visited Algeria, Sicily and Tunis. Despite limited experience he was fairly successful and his self-confidence grew. Wherever bank errands took him he used the opportunity to seek out 'brethren'. In Algiers he set up the Algerian chapter of the YMCA and distributed copies of the bible in Arabic. Inspired by reading the book by Harriet Beecher Stowe (1811–96), "Uncle Tom's Cabin" (1852), he wrote "An Account of the Regency in Tunis", a book on the geography and ethnology of North Africa which made criticism of the American slave trade. Other nations had abolished the slave trade before 1858, the year in which he published his book. It was also in this year that Henri took French dual nationality. This he did without the need to surrender his Swiss papers.

By the time Henri's employers terminated his contract in 1856, he had already formed a partnership with Henri Nick of Wurttemberg, a corn dealer and real estate agent, who was married to a niece of the Lauront Freres family, successful bankers in France. Dunant and Nick set up a corn-growing mill farm which was called 'The Financial and Industrial Company of Mons-Djemila Mills' which was near the hilltop village of Djemila close to Setif and Constantine. Nearby there were, and still are, extensive Roman archaeological remains. In order to fund this and other enterprises Henri encouraged investment from his family, their friends and associates. To this he added his recently acquired inheritance from his Aunt Sophie's Will and raised a large loan from Credit Lyonnaise.

Two years later there was a dispute with the French Algerian authorities when a French concession and a permit for a second waterfall were needed in order to turn two more pairs of watermill wheels. When the authorities became obstructive, and Henri learnt that a later applicant, a man named Rousset, had been awarded the concession for the waterfall, he set about a plan to appeal to the French Emperor Napoleon III – Louis-Napoleon Bonaparte (1808–73) in person. Friends of Dunant's family were connected to Napoleon's Chief of Staff, General de Beaufort. Together with General Dufour, who had been Napoleon's military tutor, they gained him access to General MacMahan, the French Commander-in-Chief of Algeria. Both de Beaufort and Dufour were directors and shareholders in Henri's venture. It was from General MacMahan that Henri acquired a letter of introduction to Napoleon.

To assist with his quest he wrote a book called "The Empire of Charlemagne Restored", a tribute to Napoleon, as well as a Memorandum of his company in Algeria which included a petition from its directors and important shareholders. He intended to present both exquisitely bound books to the Emperor. However, Henri's many efforts to meet with Napoleon in Paris were thwarted by officialdom, and by the summer of 1859 Napoleon was fighting with the Italians in Lombardy in a war against the Austrians.

Not to be deterred, and encouraged by General de Beaufort, Henri decided to seek an audience with Napoleon on the battlefields where he would be outside the manipulations of his Paris officials. Ignorant of the horrors of war and hoping to meet Napoleon in his hour of victory, he duly travelled to northern Italy wearing a tourist's white linen suit. At a speech he gave years later at the Geneva Convention of August 1864 he said he had been inspired to visit the battlefields by the work of Florence Nightingale.

In the Lombardo-Venetian kingdom, the Austrian Emperor Francis Joseph of the House of Hapsburg (1830–1916) led an army of 250,000 men and 400 cannons, whilst in opposition, the army of the Italian King of Sardinia, Victor Emmanuel II, together with armies of the French Emperor Napoleon III, amounted to 170,000 men with 500 cannons. The Italians wanted their land united and Napoleon supported this unification. Preceded by previous battles these armies met on 24 June 1859 near the small town of Solferino. The weather was intensely hot although later in the day there was a deluge of rain, thunder and lightning. Bugles, military bands and drums played the charges and the uniforms of the troops glistened in the sunlight. The battle became furious and bloody from the hails of shot, shell and bullets, and from the use of swords and fixed bayonets. Butchery, mutilation and death abounded and the earth became soaked with blood. The battle raged on and on with villages and fields won, then retaken repeatedly. Field hospitals carried differently coloured pennants and the cannons fired ignorantly upon them. In the shadows of the evening of this terrible day the Austrian Army retreated trying to carry away its wounded, though many thousands remained amongst the corpses of men and horses.

From a distance, and in great shock, Henri Dunant witnessed this battle and when it was over he ventured to the fields of carnage. As many as 50,000 dead soldiers and 100,000 wounded lay in pools of blood, mud and dust. Many had bones protruding, were disembowelled or were lying in an unrecognisable form. There were heart-rending cries from wounded soldiers who were writhing in agony and thirst. "Who will be able to paint the agonies of this night?" Henri asked himself, as birds of prey, vagabonds and thieves swooped.

Such was the impact of these scenes upon this man of compassion and benevolence that his revulsion and fear were overcome by the need to assist. For three days and nights without sleep, he worked alongside surviving army doctors and soldiers. He personally tended the wounded or dying, acted as interpreter, assisted at amputations, and organised local villagers, priests, nuns, landed gentry, or any tourists to become volunteers. The lack of personnel, dressings, medicines, water, food and transportation were major obstacles in this ocean of excessive need. Many dying men needed comforting or requested a letter to be sent to their loved ones. Survivors buried bodies, often anonymously. Since assistance was needed by all nationalities, as well as by prisoners of war, Henri endeavoured to promote a culture of neutrality and equality to all. Seeing Henri's adoption of no distinction of nationality, the volunteering village women and others followed his example, declaring "Tutti fratelli" – "All are brothers".

After several days of suffering from exhaustion and feelings of insufficiency to assist the many thousands in need, Henri allowed himself some time to recuperate and took a war-torn carriage in the early morning in search of the Emperor Napoleon. He found him late in the evening encamped in the town of Cavriana. "The train of war surrounding the headquarters of the Emperor of France is an imposing sight" he later wrote. He failed to get an audience with Napoleon though he was assured that his book would be presented. He withheld his Company Memorandum, preferring to leave the Emperor a plea. Shocked at what he had seen, it is possible this plea persuaded the Emperor to later issue the following orders to his soldiers: "Doctors and surgeons attached to the Austrian armies and captured while attending to the wounded shall be unconditionally released. Those who have been attending to men wounded at the Battle of Solferino and lying in the hospital at Castiglione shall, at their request, be permitted to return to Austria". Henri returned to assist in the battlefields and to help organise the movement of the wounded to hospitals in towns nearby. Many who now recognised him called him "The Man in White".

For his humanitarian work Henri Dunant received the Victor Emmanuel award of the Italian Order of St Maurice and St Lazarus in 1860, as did another Genevan, Dr Louis Appia, although the two did not meet on the battlefields. Haunted by what he had witnessed and what he felt was a 'divine call' Henri set about writing an account of his experience at Solferino and his many humanitarian ideas that emerged from this. He called his book "Un Souvenir de Solferino" – "A Memory of

Solferino". Apart from a description of his experiences, questions he asked were: "Would it be possible to establish a neutral central committee for an international aid organisation, with societies in all countries, to be ready at the time of war to assist the wounded in united action without distinction of nationality?" He also envisaged a committee that could propose a document of conventions, agreeing a basic code of behaviour in wartime, to be signed by all civilised powers. The book was published at his own expense by J G Frick of Geneva in November 1862. Initially, Henri had 1,600 copies printed which he disseminated to philanthropic groups and to high-ranking political, military, royal, aristocratic and influential figures, and newspaper editors throughout Europe. In March 1863 another four thousand were printed and the book was translated into English, Italian, Swedish and German.

In Geneva there were four well-established and influential figures who showed great interest, namely retired General Guillaume-Henri Dufour (1787–1875), Gustave Moynier, a lawyer and President of the Geneva Society for Public Welfare (1826–1910), Dr Louis Appia (1818–98) and Dr Theodore Maunoir (1806–69). These men were pious, independent and philanthropic. On 17 February 1863 these men met with Henri Dunant and it was agreed by the five to form "The International Committee for Relief to the Wounded" which was later renamed "The International Committee of the Red Cross". General Dufour was to be President, Gustave Moynier Vice-President (he was President from 1864–1910) and Henri Dunant the Secretary.

Over the ensuing months Henri put forward many ideas for debate. Amongst these were a permanent corps of trained voluntary helpers, a type of badge, a uniform, an armband or pennant, equipped and identifiable vehicles to transport the wounded, as well as well-stocked supplies of dressings, medicines and equipment. He proposed all medical and nursing staff should be given neutrality; captured military doctors and

nurses should be returned to their regiments, and there should be no distinction of nationality when dealing with the wounded and prisoners of war. He also suggested timely aid should be given to the wounded as well as the provision of interpreters, identification tags, and a tracing and communications service. He envisaged a society in every capital and, above all, a humanitarian code of conduct for all nations in war. The provision of assistance in natural disasters was added. All this was to be obtained through appeals for funding and equipment to individuals, philanthropic groups, the wealthy, royalty, the armed forces and national governments. This 'Geneva Committee of Five' had much work to do.

Henri Dunant's book was well-received internationally. His writing had the quality of the spoken word. At his own expense he hired secretaries to help him. He also spent a great deal of his own money and time undertaking an epic journey around Europe acting as an ambassador. He promoted his ideas and sought audiences with monarchs, aristocrats, influential politicians, ministers of war, the armed forces and philanthropic groups.

In Berlin in September 1863, together with a Netherlands army doctor, J H C Basting, Henri attended a Statistical Congress. Dr Basting had translated "A Memory of Solferino" into Dutch. Together they wrote a speech which Dr Basting presented in the hope that delegates, many of whom were medical men, would attend the International Committee Conference due to take place in Geneva on 23 October.

An element of Dr Basting's speech was the recommendation that countries should adopt a neutral status for the sick, the wounded, and for medical personnel in attendance on the victims of war, a proposal that had not yet been agreed upon by the Geneva Committee. Congress delegates did indeed recommend that their governments should send representatives to the forthcoming Geneva Conference. Basting and Dunant were wined and dined at Court and presented to monarchy, most of whom gave their support. Prompted by this success Dunant immediately organised the printing of a 'Berlin Circular' for distribution, to which he adhered the Committee's signature. This he did without the knowledge or agreement of his four colleagues on the Committee who were dismayed that he should have assumed this unilateral recommendation. Dr Gustave Moynier was particularly aggrieved. All, except for General Dufour, were in favour of a gradual introduction of 'neutral status', wishing not to put undue demands on governments.

Sixteen nations sent sixty-two representatives to the Geneva four-day Conference on 23 October 1863. Four came from Europe's main philanthropic institutions. The Prince of Reuss represented the Order of St John of Jerusalem. Letters of support came from the kings of Belgium, Denmark, Portugal and Russia and later from Florence Nightingale, Lord Shaftesbury and Charles Dickens. A draft Geneva Convention was made. Ten Articles were adopted including the wearing of white armbands with a red cross. The issue of neutrality was side-tracked by Moynier as Vice-Chair though Dr Basting emphatically made the point that it had much support. Henri Dunant, being a man of a nervous temperament, chose not to challenge in so huge an auditorium. His persuasive talent was in the one-to-one or smaller meeting arenas. It was the Dutchman, Dr Basting, who guided the Conference away from the conservative lawyer, Gustave Moynier.

The outcome was that supplementary clauses should be added, to the effect that neutrality be given to medical personnel and helpers, inhabitants and the wounded, and that field ambulances and hospitals should bear the universal emblem of a red cross on a white field (the 'banner of mercy'). A new movement had been created through the 'Five Founders' who now stepped onto an international platform. Swiss neutrality was stressed. Dr Basting proposed a resolution, which was adopted, acknowledging the noble ideas of Henri Dunant deserving of world-wide gratitude.

Henri Dunant continued to campaign and act as an ambassador throughout Europe and in particular, France. He gained introductions to the ambassadors of Persia and Japan and wrote to President Lincoln. This frantic activity caused him to ignore his business interests which were subconsciously plaguing him to the extent that he wrote to Gustave Moynier stating that now the International Committee was launched, he felt it was time for him to retire from the scene. Moynier disagreed, warning him this would jeopardise the success of the Five Founders' efforts.

The first Diplomatic Conference of the International Committee of the Red Cross was held in Geneva on 8 August 1864 and endorsed by Napoleon III. Henri Dunant was given the mundane task of organising the Entertainments Committee. The Americans and British sent two representatives. Agreement was reached to neutralise hospitals, field stations and medical personnel. Solid foundations were made of a legal Convention and eight Societies had already been formed. The Five Founders of the International Committee had a lot to be proud of.

In late 1864, due partly to his neglect of his business and to the amount of his personal finance he was spending on his philanthropic work, Henri Dunant's company was in desperate need of capital. French concessions had ended in 1860 and his company was unable to expand. He borrowed more money from the Genevan banks. Meanwhile, the Emperor Napoleon had nominated him Chevalier of his Legion of Honour in recognition of his Red Cross achievements. This gave Henri encouragement for the future of his Algerian ventures. The respected banker, Theodore Vernes, treasurer of the French Red Cross Society, proposed a plan to merge Dunant's company with French and foreign investors. Consequently, in May 1865 Henri was invited to a grand banquet in Algiers to commemorate Napoleon's tour of Algeria. On presentation to the Emperor he made pleas for his patronage of the French Society for the Wounded as well as for imperial protection for his new Omnium Company. Dunant took Napoleon's promises as remaining permanent. Soon after, he speculatively bought marble quarries at Felfela near Philippeville (today called Skikda) at the suggestion of his business partner, Henri Nick, who had already acquired them for half their value, though Dunant was unaware of this. Dunant sold his half-interest to Credit Genevois, a new private bank of which he was also made a director; the sum realised of 200,000 francs being the guarantee of a loan which was immediately placed to the credit of ventures being run by himself and Henri Nick, the Mills of Mons-Djemila included.

The year 1866 brought many natural calamities for Algeria; plagues, cholera, locusts, earthquakes, drought and a severe winter, causing the Paris stock exchange, the Bourse, to panic. When the Omnium Company failed Henri formed a totally Genevan enterprise, the Compagnie Algerienne, which had many prominent and respected Genevans on its Board. Still believing in the patronage of Napoleon, he hoped to collaborate or merge with similar French companies. Sadly, Dunant was unable to read the signs of the times.

In December 1866 the Credit Genevois, itself in general crisis in business, called in the loan made on the Felfela quarries to be paid in share certificates in the Compagnie Algerienne, but the share capital was not yet fully paid up. Credit Genevois went into liquidation in February 1867 and the Compagnie Algerienne, was doomed. Dunant sold all his assets in Algeria in order to pay the proceeds to reduce the loss. Mills, quarries, oak forests and gold-bearing lead mines were lost, together with the majority of his family's fortune and that of their friends and acquaintances who had invested.

Henri was bankrupt but due to continuing his philanthropic work he failed to appear at important meetings, and when he did attend he did not represent himself well. Henri and his board members were accused of mismanagement and incompetence, but not criminally so. He was disqualified as a Genevan citizen and in the public eye was blamed for the downfall of the bank even though he was not the only director involved nor the one owing the most. Henri was unable to cope with this condemnation and placed all matters into the hands of his lawyers. In March 1867 he left for Paris, never to return to Geneva for the rest of his life. The French businessman and philanthropist, Jean-Jacques Bourcart, Mayor of Buhl in the Haut-Rhin, an officer of the Academie Francaise and Chevalier of the Legion of Honour wrote to the International Committee of the Red Cross stating that Napoleon III had offered to pay half of Henri's debts so long as friends would secure the other half. He did not receive a reply. Aristocratic supporters sent money which went astray. There was a public outcry in Geneva from its very conservative and self-righteous inhabitants, Gustave Moynier amongst them, so Napoleon's idea was thwarted. Henri was unaware of his supporters' contributions nor of Napoleon's offer until he was told some thirty years later.

On 25 August 1867 Henri resigned as Secretary of the International Committee of the Red Cross and on 8 September he was fully removed as a Member. Gustave Moynier had come to loathe and rival Henri Dunant and he played a major role in his expulsion. He was also expelled from the YMCA. The Bankruptcy Court found the shareholders to be as much to blame as the directors. There was no indictment of Dunant. However, the shareholders appealed to the Court of Civil Justice who declared that Dunant had 'knowingly swindled' his colleagues by not declaring the true value of the Felfela quarries. In his memoirs he stated that he never intended to deceive anyone and that his greatest crime was to allow himself to be deceived by those he employed in Algeria who were not up to the job. He indicated he was duped and fooled by infamous French administrators. He states, "I took a hand in affairs of which I understood little and in which I was too trusting. The pain is more bitter since through my own misfortune others whom I sought to serve were involved in great losses." He also considered the French Jesuit clergy had been against him. The importance of the Felfela transaction was grossly exaggerated, it being a mere 200,000 francs. Credit Genevois had been a bank with a capital of twenty-five million francs so Dunant could not have been the main cause of its collapse. Dunant's Genevan colleagues would have been well-aware of Napoleon's promises, but to justify their investments they kept quiet in court, and Dunant was forced to sell his half of the quarries to the French Societe Algerienne company for 100,000 francs; half their true value.

Henri Dunant had earned 'the incontestable right to universal thanks' and now tragedy had befallen him. The gold medal prize of Sciences Morales at the Paris World's Fair of 1867 was not awarded to him alone, as planned, but to Moynier, Dufour and Dunant jointly so that the prize money went to the Committee as a whole; Moynier saw to that. In Paris, living in poverty, Dunant continued his humanitarian work alongside many likeminded philanthropists, some very rich, who did not ostracise him. He retained an air of respectable independence though secretly he was living in penury. He continued campaigning for the Red Cross and the French Society for the Wounded. He also campaigned for fair treatment of prisoners of war, an issue that Moynier had refused to take forward, and for disarmament negotiations. His other efforts were for an international court to mediate international conflicts and for total abolition of the slave trade. He appeared to act as a solitary ambassador for Red Cross causes, much to the chagrin of Gustave Moynier who took every opportunity to defame him.

Dunant continued to make efforts to reverse his misfortune and pay off his creditors. He frequently wrote enthusiastic letters to his mother indicating he had ideas to bring this about. He was employed by an Italian, Max Grazia, as the secretary of his newly-formed World Library although the remuneration was meagre. A major idea, which had been on his mind for several years, prompted by some of the many campaigners and businessmen he met, both Zionists and Protestants, was to seek concessions from ruling Turkey for land in Palestine to develop; thereafter to be colonised by Jews, some of whom had already settled there. He wrote a brochure entitled "Renovation de l'Orient" which he had presented to the Sultan of the Ottoman Empire when he was attending the Paris World's Fair. From this commercial enterprise he considered he could make hundreds of millions of francs, as did other businessmen and aristocrats. Dunant's vision of the restoration of the Holy Land to Christian safekeeping did not materialise. He waited in vain for any news of an agreement from Turkey.

Henri kept a constant correspondence with his mother. Later that year she came to visit him in Paris bringing the much needed clothing he had left at home. He drew great strength from her support and encouragement to find ways of paying his debts. They stayed at the Hotel Meurice from where they explored Paris together, but these were to be his last days of maternal warmth and closeness. In early 1868 Henri's mother's health failed and she died. Henri was devastated and distraught, for his soul had been closest to her. His exile and his lack of funds for travel prevented his attendance at her funeral.

It was at this time that Henri met Madame Leonie Kastner (1820–88), the widow of musician Jean-Georges Kastner. Leonie Kastner was wealthy in her own right, having inherited from her father, Jean-Francois Boursault, actor, theatre director, businessman and French revolutionary. She lent Henri her house for meetings and for modest fees he helped in tutoring her son, Frederic. Their friendship was close, perhaps the only close adult relationship of his life. In his memoirs he states that he believed she loved him but that he dared not approach her since he was heavily in debt and ruined. He admitted to a passionate attachment and amorous friendship with profound respect. Madame Kastner helped Henri in many ways, at times keeping him from starvation, although with difficulty because he would refuse charity. Repayment had to be made from the allocation of 'tasks'.

In 1870 France was involved in a war with the Prussians. After a short-lived battle at Sedan, which culminated in defeat for the French, Napoleon capitulated and was held as a prisoner of war at Wilhelmshohe in Prussia. By the time of his release France had declared a Republic. Consequently, he chose to be exiled to England. Two German armies besieged Paris and the Prussians established their headquarters at Versailles. With the fall of their Empire a Third French Republic was proclaimed but whilst still fighting the Germans the French became embroiled in their own revolution. Dunant tried another commercial venture. He and a Dr Cheron manufactured lint for the wounded, impregnated to prevent sepsis. The business initially did well but ultimately failed. However, his humanitarian spirit prevailed. He acted as a 'scarlet pimpernel' in assisting those fleeing Paris and made representations to political figures, pleading for them to recognise the Geneva Conventions. His hectic life now involved assisting or organising help for the wounded. The British Red Cross sent aid to the French and to the Prussians.

The Germans and Prussians proclaimed the German Empire at Versailles on 18 January 1871. On 29 January an armistice was signed with the French to last three weeks and the Germans sent provisions into Paris to relieve the acute food shortage. Help was also sent from New York and London. The French Red Cross requested Dunant act as an intermediary for the saving of lives and objects of art, which he did successfully. On 26 February a Peace Treaty was signed between France and Germany, France having conceded Alsace and East Lorraine to the Germans, together with five billion francs. It was agreed they would also release their French military prisoners of war to enable them to assist in fighting the revolutionaries. In Paris a revolutionary and socialist government known as the 'Paris Commune' ruled

until 28 May but after its downfall, over twenty thousand workers, revolutionaries and anarchists were executed and thousands were deported to the penal colony of New Caledonia. To Henri's nightmares of Solferino were added the siege, the Commune and its aftermath.

In March of 1872 Henri gathered together those who shared his views, including the pacifist Frederic Passy and humanitarians, the Comte de Flavigny, whom he had helped to escape to England, and Ferdinand de Lesseps, developer of the Suez Canal. They founded the World Alliance for Order and Civilisation. This put him dangerously into the areas of pacifism and international arbitration as alternatives to war, though there was no revolutionary spirit within him and he feared anarchy. The fair treatment of prisoners of war was also on its agenda. The humanitarian Leonie Kastner put her personal wealth to this cause and her only son Frederic, a physicist, assumed the post of secretary.

On the subject concerning the treatment of prisoners of war, Henri was invited to speak in London at the Social Science Association and Brighton's Royal Pavilion where he was well-received. Florence Nightingale wrote to him stating 'noble work – work truly inspired by God'. Moynier's malicious act of sending a copy of the Geneva Bankruptcy Court decision to the London society made no difference to his popularity. Even though the Dukes of Wellington, Norfolk, Somerset and Sutherland agreed to become honorary patrons, the British Government rejected the idea of convening a diplomatic conference. The causes for prisoners of war did not raise the same interest as the wounded on the battlefields. Dunant, now spelling Henry with a 'y', planned a conference in Paris but it never took place, mainly due to the fact that the Tsar of Russia had organised one in Brussels. The London Anti-Slavery Society paid Henry's fare to attend.

Even with such high-ranking support and an appeal by General Gordon in the British press, the 'Alliance' failed to attract the donations required.

Henry's missionary spirit returned however, and with a small loan from his brother, Pierre, who was now a successful doctor in Geneva, he returned to England in the summer of 1872 where he campaigned vigorously in high places and lectured in London, Plymouth, Liverpool, Manchester and other cities. However, Henry's health was beginning to fail him. Five years of poor nutrition was taking its toll causing problems with his digestion. He also had eczema of his right hand and a severe anxiety from financial worries and pressures from his creditors and enemies. At this time Madame Leonie Kastner, an ardent Bonapartist, and her son Frederic were in England. Henry achieved an audience for them to meet with Napoleon who was living at Camden Place in Chislehurst. Henry considered this a part repayment for the kindness she had shown him.

Henry acquired a small income from working as secretary of the Peace Society of London and the National Association for the Promotion of Social Science. Though subscriptions were not large enough to sustain him, he lectured and campaigned tirelessly. He appealed for Napoleon's support. They were now both exiles in the same land. Louis Napoleon did indeed endorse Henry's aims, which he put in writing. Henry Dunant at long last had a document of imperial endorsement from his 'fabulous' Emperor. Louis Napoleon III died in Surrey on 9 January 1873 following an operation for gall stones. He is entombed in St Michael's Abbey in Farnborough, together with his wife Empress Eugenie (1826–1920), and their only child, Prince Napoleon Eugene Louis Bonaparte (1856–79), who had joined the British Royal Artillery and was killed fighting in the Anglo-Zulu War. This was the end of that Bonaparte line.

The eczema of Henry's right hand worsened and it appears he took a job, possibly teaching languages, in the employ of a Mrs Coombes who ran a girls' boarding school in Flodden Road, Camberwell. She tended his ailments and gave him shelter at her home 'Broadlands'. He was still campaigning amongst the rich and famous and even met the Shah of Persia at a reception in Buckingham Palace, although he had to attend wearing less than pristine clothes. Madame Kastner continued to allocate 'tasks' for him from Paris and Strasbourg and asked him to promote her son's invention of the pyrophone, an organ-like instrument fuelled by gas flames. Although Henry put great effort into organising talks and demonstrations of this instrument he had no aptitude for music nor science. Only his poverty and loyalty drove him. (There is a pyrophone in the Science Museum placed there by Dunant.) Feelings of persecution and bitterness began to plague him. Henry accompanied Madame Kastner acting as 'courier' for her near year-long expedition to Venice and Rome but he was tormented by fears of his ambiguous position when he overheard spurious comments or outright condemnation. Madame Kastner insisted he spend his 'task-earned' money treating his eczema at spas. One of these was in the little Swiss resort village of Heiden in Appenzell above St Gallen on Lake Constance. For Henry this brought back soothing memories of his youth in Geneva. The lake is partly in Switzerland and Austria, with a larger part in Germany. It is just a hundred miles south from Stuttgart.

Back in London Henry continued to earn small amounts working for various humanitarian societies, undertaking paid research or translations. He was for a time on the Isle of Wight and at Weston-super-Mare. His suspicions of connivance and vengeance blurred with his demons and senses of injustice. His Genevan enemies were constantly spreading spurious rumours which at times prevented his employment. During 'the Commune' in Paris the rumours had been that he was a Prussian spy, that he was funded by Napoleon, or that he was a communist, and it was suggested that he had a rich mistress in Madame Kastner. A lawyer representing Credit Genevois visited him in Paris, forcing him to sign an undertaking giving them prior claim on any of his earnings until his debts were paid. His vitality was failing him and he was fading into obscurity.

Even Madame Kastner's benevolence dissolved when her son Frederic became embroiled with a woman who convinced them that Dunant was to blame for the commercial failure of the pyrophone invention. Leonie Kastner then began to withdraw her contact. Frederic found sanctuary in alcohol and died in 1882 after which his mother gradually severed her links with Henry.

In Stuttgart, Henry sought refuge with Pastor Dr Ernst Rudolph Wagner (1808–78) who was president of a charitable organisation and had translated his "Memory of Solferino" into German. Whilst out walking in Stuttgart, by chance he met the Tubingen University student Rudolf Muller and they became friends. When Dr Wagner died, Henry intermittently lived in the house of his widow, Ida, until she died in 1885. It is believed he travelled for various charities to Italy, Germany, France and London but he lived in poverty, was disillusioned, depressed and feeling persecuted.

In his memoirs, Henry refers to his exhaustion and the spiritual pain and misery of living in poverty, with a poor diet, threadbare clothes, sodden shoes or sleeping in the waiting-rooms of big railway stations. This was his lowest point. In 1887 he wrote from Stuttgart to his brother, Pierre, describing his life. It appears this Genevan medical branch of the family were united by this letter and decided that the man who had founded the Red Cross could not be left to destitution. Accordingly, they decided to allocate him twelve hundred francs a year. At last, his existence, though still frugal, could be more secure.

Consequently, in July of that year Henry moved to live in a small, cheap room in the Pension Paradiso at Heiden from where he had views of the mountains and Lake Constance. He could just afford pencils and paper for writing to Pierre, Marie his surviving sister, and to a niece and nephews. Henry had few visitors save for Rudolph Muller (1856–1922) now a professor, who visited him yearly from Stuttgart and was writing the first account of "The Origins of the Red Cross". A Dr Altherr treated his chronic eczema, and the village teacher, William Sonderegger and his wife, Susanna, befriended him and encouraged him to write his memoirs. Susanna founded a branch of the Red Cross in Heiden in 1890 and Henry became its honorary president. On learning that the International Red Cross Conference was to be held in Rome in April 1892, Henry encouraged William Sonderegger to attend, but William had neither the time nor funds to do so. Since Henry's disappointment was so great, William drafted a note for the Conference outlining Henry's situation. Members of the Red Cross were amazed to learn that he was still alive. The Sondereggers and Henry were deluged with correspondence offering help. One in particular came from the section of the Red Cross based at Winterthur just north of Zurich which was led by its clerk, a schoolmaster, Johann Pfister. However, from the International Committee in Geneva the hand of reconciliation was not forthcoming.

That year Henry, aged sixty-four, moved to lodge in two austere but bright rooms in Dr Altherr's small nursing home in Heiden where he remained for the last eighteen years of his life. His mood swings began to plague him, one day he was sociable, the next day irritable, depressed, or paranoid, to the extent that he suspected his food was being poisoned. He felt persecuted, betrayed and forgotten but he still pressed ahead with writing his memoirs, at times erratically. He also renounced his Christian beliefs.

In the summer of 1895, Georg Baumberger, a journalist from a St Gallen newspaper, learnt of Henry. On discovering that he was the founder of the International Committee of the Red Cross, he wrote a small article calling him "The Hermit of Heiden" and offered to interview him more fully. Henry felt rejuvenated by the opportunity to speak. He also provided pages from his memoirs, letters from Europe's royal families, Napoleon III, Gladstone and Florence Nightingale, as well as other documents. A photographer was sent and in September Georg Baumberger published an article locally entitled "Henri Dunant, the Founder of the Red Cross" which was reprinted by more major Swiss and German newspapers and henceforth across Europe. A new generation was now reading his story of Solferino.

At the age of sixty-eight Henry Dunant had been rediscovered and the response was overwhelming. A multitude of tributes, visits, awards and donations were made to him. Letters arrived from former royal supporters, the Russian tsarist widow Maria Feodorovna provided a pension, and a signed photograph arrived from Pope Leo XIII. Swiss and foreign dignitaries visited; the pacifist Bertha von Suttner, founder of the Austrian Society of Friends of Peace and a member of the Austro-Hungarian nobility, visited and started a correspondence with him. The fame consoled his soul for it gave him an opportunity to gain acknowledgment for being the founder of the International Committee of the Red Cross and originator of the Geneva Conventions. It also renewed his energies to write about and support ideas for peace and philanthropic causes.

Gustave Moynier was not pleased. He had erased Dunant's name from the official history of the Red Cross and requests for official photographs of him were turned down. However, when Moynier demanded that the Committee do something to oppose Dunant's regained fame, they voted to do nothing. Moynier was to endure further anguish when in 1901 it was revealed that in the Will of Alfred Nobel (1833–96) there was to be a provision for a Peace Prize and that Henry Dunant's name had been submitted. By 1897 Professor Rudolf Muller's book about the origins of the Red Cross, which contradicted the official history and espoused Dunant's role, had been read widely, in particular by Dr Hans Daae, the Norwegian military physician who then advocated Dunant's case to the Nobel Committee. Amongst others, the name of the French pacifist, Frederic Passy (1822–1912) had also been put forward. Rather than submit Gustave Moynier's name, who had in fact successfully devoted many years of his life to the cause, the International Committee of the

Red Cross decided to submit neither Moynier's name nor the Committee as a whole.

In the event, the first Nobel Peace Prize was awarded in 1901 jointly to Henry Dunant and Frederic Passy. Henry was too frail to attend the ceremony. Dr Hans Daae arranged for Dunant's prize money of 104,000 Swiss Francs to be deposited in a Norwegian bank to avoid access by his creditors. Henry Dunant never spent any of this money but when he died in 1910 aged eighty-two, he left legacies to his carers, to friends who had helped him in Stuttgart, and to charities in Norway and Switzerland. Remaining funds were left to his creditors to partially relieve his debt which was a major burden to him until his death. His memoirs and papers were bequeathed to his nephew, Maurice, and are now stored in the Archives of the University of Geneva.

Henry Dunant died on Sunday 30 October 1910. In accordance with his wishes 'to be carried to my grave like a dog', the next day the carpenter from the village transported his plain wooden coffin on a handcart. The church bell tolled but there was no funeral, no flowers and no mourners. Only a small boy approached walking home from school. He was William Sonderegger's son, Rene. In 1935 Rene wrote a book "Jean Henri Dunant, Revolutionar" in which he recalls:

> "The waves of sound from the bell swept like a faint breeze over that strangely simple last journey of this great man, heir of the ancient covenanters of Switzerland. That humble leave-taking of a heart that had encompassed the world, occupied my imagination for years. My unbounded youthful hatred of injustice and baseness led me to make wandering journeys the world over, but whenever my mind turned towards home, there in its depths, was the secret of that encounter".

Henry Dunant was cremated in Zurich where there is now a memorial at the Friedhof Sihlfeld Cemetery. His birthday, 8 May, is World Red Cross and Red Crescent Day and the former nursing home in Heiden has become the Henry Dunant Museum. Worldwide, there are many memorials, places, streets and schools named after him, and there is a Henry Dunant Medal awarded every two years. The headquarters of the International Committee of the Red Cross remains in Geneva where there is also a Museum and an extensive Archive. The Red Cross is the largest humanitarian network in the world with one hundred and eighty-nine National Societies.

The International Red Cross and Red Crescent Movement has seven Fundamental Principles, the first of which 'Humanity' is:

"The International Red Cross and Red Crescent Movement, born of a desire to bring assistance without discrimination to the wounded on the battlefield, endeavours – in its international and national capacities – to prevent and alleviate suffering wherever it may be found. Its purpose is to protect life and health and to ensure respect for every human being. It promotes mutual understanding, friendship, cooperation and lasting peace amongst all peoples."

On 6 October 2014, as an added recognition of Henry Dunant's achievements, Switzerland's second highest mountain was renamed 'Dunantspitze' – 'Peak Dunant'.

Henry Dunant, 1908. Courtesy of the British Red Cross.

SECTION ONE
THE TWO VIENNAS

CHAPTER ONE
THE EARLY LIFE OF MR EDWARD JAMES FREESTONE

WHEN EDWARD JAMES FREESTONE was born at Garton Road, Southampton in June 1918, five months before the end of the First World War, neither his mother, Alice née Tappin aged thirty nor his father, James Freestone, aged forty-four, could have envisaged the fate that would befall their newly-born son twenty-two years later.

James Freestone had been widowed twice in Byker, Newcastle Upon Tyne. Times were hard, wages low and life expectancy short. He left his daughters, Marjory and Mary-Elizabeth, by his second wife, to be cared for by aunts when he sought work in the ship-building industry in Barrow-in-Furness. Here he married for a third time and had a son, Harold or Harry. When work again became scarce he left both wife and son behind and went in search of employment in far away Southampton. According to the 1911 Census James Freestone was 'single', an 'anglesmith' and boarding at 12 St Johns Road, Woolston, Southampton. He gave his age as thirty years although he was in fact thirty-seven.

Alice Tappin met James Freestone soon after this time. Their first child, Alice Edith, known as Edith, was born in early 1913 at Garton Road. They went on to produce Thomas William, known as Will, in 1916, Edward James (the subject of my story, known as Eddie, Ted or Teddy) in 1918, and Robert in 1921. A younger son, Joseph was born and died in 1924.

Edward grew up with his parents, his siblings and his maternal grandmother, Mary Tappin, née Lee; her husband, Thomas Edward Tappin having died in 1919. They rented the three-bedroomed house at 1 Surrey Road, Woolston. The Tappins were from Chiswick. Like so many families after the turn of the century, they had moved to Southampton seeking work in the ship-building industry.

I recorded the life of Edward James Freestone when he was sixty-nine years old.

MY FATHER WAS A proper 'Geordie'. He was a blacksmith-anglesmith and striker at Thorneycroft's where they built all the big liners in those days. He went off to work very early in the mornings to do the hard work of making big fitments and propellers for the ships. Like others in those days, he worked six days a week and unfortunately, to compensate, this led to many of them becoming heavy drinkers and gamblers. Gambling was a sore point with my mother. Sometimes my father would finish work on a Saturday, be paid, come home with a few of his mates, bringing a few pints of beer, and they would sit down to play cards and gamble. These 'sessions' could last from Saturday night until early Monday morning – drinking, smoking and gambling for up to thirty-six hours! My mother used to go 'spare' because the household money got lost or was reduced.

My father owned several whippet dogs which he used to race nearby on Peartree Green. This was a lovely green park then and we children used to have to stand at one end of the green holding white handkerchiefs which we waved to start the races. At the other end of the green my father, uncles and other owners would then let the whippets loose. That was one of our Sunday entertainments.

As we grew a little older my brothers and I used to go fishing on the beach on Weston Shore, or, with our friends, we'd dare one another to swim across the estuary where the river flows into Southampton Water. We could swim like fish. There were times when we'd climb up the inside of the disused tall chimney of the old rolling mills. To us it was a fantastic jungle of adventure. I had an older friend called Sam who used to be a skipper on yachts. He skippered the 'Endeavour' for Lord Tommy Sopwith and, of course, I used to go out sailing with him when he wasn't doing any competitive racing. I could also fish from the yacht and take home a fish or two which were valuable to my family at that time. I spent many hours on the 'Endeavour' which was a world class winner.

Sometimes on Sundays we'd spend time with our mother, friends and neighbours. We'd take a pram full of goodies for our picnic and walk the shore road to Netley. When I say 'neighbours' I mean three or four big families from our street – the Cockerells, the Lindows or the Irish McLaughlans and others. We'd picnic and then play football on the beach. We were all very friendly. Actually, when I was due to go abroad at the start of the Second World War Mrs McLaughlan, being a Catholic, gave me a crucifix which I still have. She said to me "This will protect you during the War" and whether it did or not I don't know but I wore it throughout the War and I survived!

Often, of course, we'd go to Sunday school at St Mark's Church. We'd even get to go on school and church outings where we would be given a banana, an orange and an apple in a bag and taken by bus to somewhere in the countryside. Also, when I was about twelve, my school selected me for a trip to the 'open air' school at Stubbington, Lee-on-Solent. Just so many of us were chosen and sent for a fortnight under canvas. We explored the

seashore, studied the biology of the plants and we also studied the weather. I won a pen and pencil for being a good student there. It was quite enjoyable. In the winter season when the snow fell heavily we used to slide on our sledges down the hill of Lake Road. Oh yes, we had lovely times!

I attended Western Boys' School, which was then in Florence Road until it was bombed in the Second World War. We had good tuition because we could all read, write, do arithmetic, geography, history and, of course, art. We had devoted but strict teachers. We were not allowed to stay home from school unless we were severely ill. Before we could move up to another class we had to complete our studies in the class below, perfecting everything. We never left school with any high qualifications but we had a good educational grounding. We were all capable of taking exams for the Grammar Schools but unfortunately my mother couldn't afford to keep us in the type of school with a special uniform to buy, it was a bit out of her reach.

When I was fourteen my father died, which broke my heart. I then certainly couldn't go on to higher education. He died from cancer of the lower jaw aged fifty years though I now believe he was actually fifty-eight. By this time my mother had three jobs. She took in washing early in the day, then mornings and lunch-times she was in charge of the 'Steel Room' of Plummer Roddis department store at the top of the Southampton High Street. In their restaurant she had to attend to all the silver cutlery, making sure it was presentable and clean. At the end of the afternoon she cleaned the offices of the Friendly Insurance Society in London Road.

When I left school at fourteen my mother managed to get me a three-year apprenticeship in the bakery at Plummer Roddis training to become a pastry chef and confectioner. My brother, Will, who was two years older than me was also there undertaking an apprenticeship as a chef. All the staff used to call my mother 'Mum' because Will and I did! Comedians used to joke about it on the stage of the Palace and Empire theatres, we were that well-known. I was working with the confectionery for the very large restaurant which was on the top floor. It was open all day and there was a big orchestra playing all sorts of lovely music. We made buns, scones, dough-nuts, gateaux and fresh cream cakes. I was taught how to make all that. My apprenticeship included training in the evenings – one evening at Lankester and Crook's bakery, one evening at Lowman's bakery and one evening of theory at the Deanery School to learn art, design, costings, book-keeping, and presentation – we had to learn it all. I earned ten shillings a week right throughout my apprenticeship which I used to give to my mother for my keep. She would give me two shillings and sixpence back, which is 25p today, and with that I used to buy my clothes and save.

Cakes made by Edward Freestone.

Edward Freestone with his mother in Woolston, early 1930s.

In 1932 Plummer Roddis was a marvellous place to work. I even learnt to make beautiful baskets of roses out of marzipan icing and they were put on display in the restaurant where the food was of very high quality. If you shopped or ate at Plummer's in those days you were considered almost the upper class.

At the end of my apprenticeship in 1935 the manageress told me I was now too good to stay and advised me to get another job to gain more experience. My brother, Will, having already completed his apprenticeship, had left

Plummer's and was working as a chef in a big hotel called the Caledonian in Piccadilly Circus, London. He was gaining experience from Italian, French and Indian chefs. When Joe Louis the famous boxer came to London my brother became his personal chef. He would not have anyone else, and for all his wonderful cooking Joe Louis gave Will signed photographs of himself and other famous boxers.

Whilst waiting for a job to become available at the large department store called Adderley's in Leicester I took a temporary job at New Ideal Picture film studios canteen in Hammersmith, London where I made all the cakes, bread and rolls for the whole studio. There were quite a few famous people working there. I met Sandy Powell, Googie Withers and another young lady who was killed during the War when she was on stage and a bomb dropped directly on her. Her name was Margaret Millison and she was engaged to Fred Perry, the famous tennis player. She was a lovely young girl. She used to talk to me about making cakes and confectionery.

I collected lots of photographs signed by famous actors and actresses but when I was away at War my landlady in Leicester sent my clothes and belongings home to my mother in Southampton. Sadly, that suitcase was bombed at Southampton railway station so everything was lost, including my collection of signed photographs and my City and Guilds Certificates – all lost in the air raid – a lot of treasured things gone.

The job in Leicester finally came up in March 1936 and I went to work at Adderley's Department Store which was on the same footing as Plummer Roddis in Southampton. It belonged to the Marshall and Snelgrove Group. It was a large store where three hundred ladies and twenty men were employed. At one stage I lived in a guest house nearby in London Road which meant I could walk to work. The quality and standards of the store were very high and the people I met there were very nice. It was a place where lords and ladies came to be fitted for their clothes. It was very exclusive. In the elegant restaurant, which had pink décor, an orchestra played and models walked, displaying furs, hats and gowns.

Some of the staff I worked with were quite talented. We used to play tennis, cricket and do a lot of swimming, both before and after work. Sometimes we'd go to the Grand Hotel for a drink and even have oysters. With my friends from the Gentlemen's Department I attended a lot of operas and symphony concerts at the Leicester de Montfort Hall. I heard some famous artists sing and play. I wasn't educated in music but I used to listen to a radio programme called 'Housewives' Choice' on which both popular and classical pieces were played. I thought how beautiful it was. It appealed to my feelings and when friends in Leicester suggested I go with them to symphonies, operas, ballets or shows, I became very interested. Whilst I was a Prisoner of War I became really interested – but that's another story!

I remember when 'Hiawatha' was being staged I carved Hiawatha's head from a large block of chocolate which looked so impressive that my boss put it on display in the restaurant – it was great advertising for the show. By this time my wage had jumped to three pounds a week but I used to send home ten shillings a week to help out my mother.

I had girlfriends at this time but nothing serious. I knew some nice ladies amongst the staff, one of whom named Margaret, used to sing opera. I had another friend who also worked in Adderley's whose name was

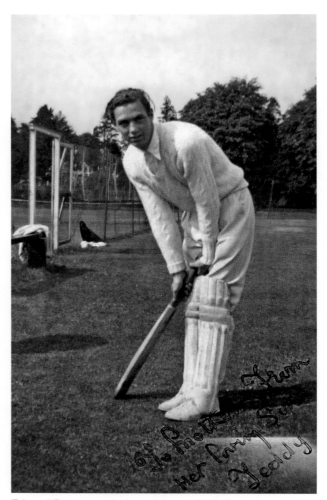

Edward Freestone playing cricket 1937, Leicester.

Henrietta who came from a mining area in Leicestershire called Coalville. Her father used to entertain me and even took me down a mine but what I admired about this man was that he saved all his hard-earned money to have his daughter taught the violin. She played beautifully, I'll always remember that. There was nothing serious in our friendship. It wasn't until ten years after the War that I had a serious girlfriend and got married.

Now and again I spent weekends at home with my mother in Southampton. I used to have to save to do this but it was a great joy, after being in the Midlands industrial city of Leicester, to come to Southampton to catch the breath of fresh air down here, the sea air, lovely it was; lovely! I used to enjoy that.

I also had a colleague with whom I became very friendly who worked in the high class Funeral Undertaking Department of Adderley's. He used to dress in top hat, black jacket, low-frock tails and striped trousers. Even I had to wear a pinstriped suit at work at certain times. He was a Roman Catholic and he took me to a place outside Leicester called Flitwick Monastery where in our spare time we studied Catholicism with the monks. I did this for a year or so but in the end found it too demanding and gave up.

However, my friend sent to Rome for a small painting of St Boniface on a handkerchief particularly blessed by the Pope, which he gave to me. It's said the original still hangs in the Vatican today. Lots of painters used to go there to copy the imprint. The story is, as Jesus was carrying his cross to be crucified, Veronica stepped out of the crowd and gave him a handkerchief to wipe his face and the impression of his face was left on it. As you look at the painting on my handkerchief the eyes of the face appear to open and close. To get this effect the painters used forty-seven different colours. I'll always treasure that handkerchief because it came with me throughout the War.

Edward Freestone. Pinstriped suit for certain days at work. Adderley's Department Store, Leicester, 1936–39.

The crucifix given by his neighbour and kept with Edward Freestone throughout the War.

25

CHAPTER TWO
THE SECOND WORLD WAR BEGINS

IT WAS IN 1938 when Hitler's power was ascending that things got very scary. My friends and I felt we ought to be doing something about this so we went to the Territorial Army Office (TA) in Leicester and joined up as Volunteers in the 2nd Leicestershire TA Unit.

Being in the TA meant that we trained at South Wigston Army Barracks on two or three evenings a week after we'd finished work. Here we learnt to keep fit, to march and to put together machine guns, hand guns and rifles. We were also sent for a fortnight to a basic training camp at Hollyhead in North Wales where we learnt how to fire a gun and how to get on with other people, I suppose.

During total war the Territorial Army in Britain was incorporated into the Regular Service. Mr Edward Freestone's TA training had included leadership and combat training skills. Consequently, in war-time he was given the NCO (Non-Commissioned Officer) rank of Corporal in the Regular Service. Corporal was a step up from Lance Corporal. The NCO Corps, as primary and most visible leaders of military personnel, became the backbone of the armed forces. In addition, they were responsible for carrying out a military organisation's mission and training. Once War was declared Edward Freestone became Corporal Edward James Freestone in the 2/5 Battalion of the Leicestershire Regiment, 46th Division.

We were issued with khaki battle-dress, trousers and boots. Then, as an emergency measure, with War looming, I was actually called up to the Leicestershire Regiment in the Summer of 1939. My quality of work as a pastry chef and confectioner was very high and since I didn't wish to lower it I insisted I didn't want to become an Army cook. I opted for the plain Infantry and that's where they put me.

I had to report to a disused shoe factory on the river bank in Ullswater Road, Leicester where at night we just slept on the oily floor. When things became more organised we were given civilian billets. We walked along a road and our superior would knock on any door requesting they take in two soldiers. Everyone was very nice to us.

We stayed in billets until we were called to France in early 1940. We were inoculated and put on a train to Southampton Docks where we waited for a boat to come alongside. Once on the boat we moored off Hythe Pier for twenty-four hours because there was a submarine scare in the English Channel. At the time I said to my friend "I'd only have to swim across Southampton Water as I did as a kid, and I'd be home to see my mother!"

However, that was not to be and we eventually slipped anchor and moved across to France and landed at Cherbourg, with our land destination being Rennes in Northern Brittany – the beautiful city of Rennes. As well as doing heavy training here we had the freedom to go out into Rennes. I made friends with a young French girl whose parents owned a hotel and I used to go there for meals.

Rennes today.

After a few months, towards May 1940, we had a sudden order to pull up camp and go to an unknown destination. We were put on trains and shunted here and there. The Germans were bombing us all the time. At a place in France called Seclin our train was bombed and tripped off the line. I was trapped by girders lying across my legs but I was eventually freed. No bones were broken but I had big dents in my ankles. Once the train was back on the line we were moved right up to the Albert Canal in Belgium.

It was here that we came under heavy attack from the Germans. There was one bridge over the Albert Canal that King Leopold would not allow to be blown up so that's where the Germans came across. The British Artillery was ordered to withdraw but not to leave anything behind, so we pumped enough ammunition in six hours to last a fortnight, everything we had. I didn't end up with the people I enlisted with. Not only that, at the last minute young men we called 'immaturists' were called up to make up the number of Reserves – sixteen or seventeen year olds they were, and had never fired a rifle. I was teaching them on the front line how to fire a rifle! Then we had to start falling back – by foot, there was no transport.

There was also the matter of conducting Refugees whose numbers were terrific; thousands and thousands of women and children, pushchairs, pregnant women, old people – all marching along the road. It was impossible to move up, so we had to try to control them to one side. And all the time we were being bombed. There were a lot of casualties. Of course, because of lack of supplies the majority of the troops were flooding back towards Dunkirk, that's where they were retreating to.

We withdrew eventually to a place called Le Bassée just south of Lille in Northern France where we had to 'dig in'. I was in a little 'dug out' at the forward line overlooking the Le Bassée Canal. Le Bassée is basically a coal-mining area, so our dug-outs soon turned to coal-dust and started to bury us each time a

bomb landed. As one of the more experienced, I had a Bren gun but when I called for more ammunition I got machine-gun munitions which didn't fit Bren guns, so I was finished. It all happened so quickly because the supplies brought to us were useless. There was plenty of German opposition – they just came across the Le Bassée Canal in black rubber dinghies and we just tried to lay them down, but after our ammunition was gone there was nothing we could do. We were also being shelled with mortars. Our orders were to stay there and fight to the last man. There was no-one to pick up the wounded and we had had no food for two or three days – there was no means of getting it to us because behind us there were two wide canals.

Le Bassée Canal today, near Lille, France.

Eventually, the Officer of my C Company, Captain Clarke, came to me and said "Corporal Freestone, I'm afraid it's everyone to the last man" so I turned around to the boys and said "That's it". The Germans came around to the right and behind us, encircling us. The next thing I heard was "Schlus, schlus, hein, hein". We were absolutely out-numbered and out-witted with no ammunition. The Germans had great Lugers in their hands. I just said "OK, fair enough". I can't describe what a terrible feeling that was to see another fighting man armed to the teeth with Lugers and pistols shaking at you. We just had to put our hands up and say we were British soldiers and that was all there was to it. We had to surrender.

Tributary of Le Bassée Canal near Seclin, France.

There were about four left from my Platoon and I saw my young friend machine-gunned right through the tummy. I haven't forgotten that. I never will. We were all rounded up and there were quite a few from my Company. We were then transported across the canal, all lined up against a wall and a machine gun was put ready. This was about 10 o'clock in the morning. The Sergeant-Major, grand old boy who had fought in the First World War, said to me "Well, I think this is it". I found it hard to think. What can you think when you are so frightened?

However, all of a sudden a smart-looking German officer came round the corner of a big building at the side and put his foot on the German machine-gunner and pushed him to one side. How that happened I really don't know but I can only surmise by reading books about it afterwards. It was either a tactic to frighten us into submission or, contrary to the past, Hitler had ordered that nobody was to be shot because at the time he wanted to negotiate a Peace Treaty with Britain.

Captain Clarke who had told us to fight to the last man – how he got back I shall never know – he came back and sent a letter to my mother telling her he had seen me killed in action – and my mother received that letter! She only found out that I was still alive when the Red Cross was able to contact her about a year later telling her I was a Prisoner of War. I can see how it happened though because we were trapped between two very wide canals. I would have swam across one of those canals but our orders were to fight to the last ammunition. We were under very heavy and accurate fire. I assume he thought we must all have died in a small place like that.

After our close escape from being machine-gunned we were herded together at the top of a mineshaft. The mines in this area were quite close together and the pit-heads contained big sheds, and that's where the Germans temporarily placed us. Then gradually they marched us off behind their lines. I think this was the 27th or 28th of May. We were then forced-marched to Poland. I think it was something like 860 miles. I walked the whole way!

The likely route from Le Bassée would have been through Lille in France to Liege in Belgium, then into Germany to Aachen, Cologne, Dortmund, Hanover, North Berlin and further North to Stettin, then East to Marienburg in Poland and ultimately South to Torun.

28

CHAPTER THREE
IMPRISONMENT IN POLAND

THE GERMANS HAD MILITARY transport but we were force-marched because there were so many of us. We marched quite a few miles, day and night, but as we had little food we became less active and consequently we couldn't do the night marching. Where we stopped we slept, in a field or wherever, and in whatever type of weather, out in the open. There were some field kitchens where watery soup was issued but, of course, there were so many prisoners that it took an age to get a drop. When breakfast-time was over some of us just didn't get any if we weren't lucky enough to get to the front of the queue. We just had to keep marching on and picking up what we could along the way. In France and Belgium there were fruit trees along the roads and there was always some fruit to pick and eat. Marching through Germany and into Poland was not so easy. These lonely roads had metalled surfaces but when military convoys came along we were thrown off the road and into the woods so they could pass by. Looking back, I don't know how we walked so far along those lonely, lonely roads into Poland.

I can't assess how many prisoners died along the way but there were soldiers continually falling out and collapsing with exhaustion. We just plodded on and kept in groups with our own particular Regimental Company as much as we could. We tried to help one another. That was one of the amazing things about it. As others fell down we had to try to help. The spirit to help was marvellous.

It took us until the end of September to get to a big fort in Polish territory. It was very large with underground dungeons surrounded by a big dry moat. The fort towered sixty feet above the moat and we were initially shut up in its dungeons. We entered by being marched across a big bridge crossing the moat. I say 'marched' but many of us actually had to crawl on our hands and knees, we were so weak. As we were crossing the bridge the Germans were evacuating many Jewish women who were almost naked with shaven heads. We did not know about the extermination camps then and we wondered how the Germans could treat people so inhumanely.

Bridge and moat within Marienburg Castle (Malbork today), northern Poland. Part of the Castle was Stalag XXB.

From this camp we were sent out to undertake hard labour in 'working parties'. I was selected on several occasions for a 'working

Lonely road in Poland today, travelling East.

29

party' to go to the port of Danzig (Gdansk). Our job there was to build up the roads leading towards the big German military headquarters and that's what we were doing – laying roads; very heavy work.

Steps to dungeons, Marienburg Castle, Stalag XXB.

It was about this time that I heard about a couple of prisoners who had escaped from their working party. They had escaped by falling to the ground, rolling themselves in the mud and dirt, lying still and then later disappearing into nearby trees. After eventually arriving right at the port, they chose to stow away on a boat where the captain was fortunately sympathetic to the British. He hid them on board and they eventually got back to Britain. I wonder if they had prior knowledge of this 'sympathetic' captain. This true story set me thinking about a means of escape.

It was here that I became friendly with one or two British Quaker prisoners. One of these was named Alan Hutchison. He was a lovely man who was teaching me Spanish. He had been a professor of Spanish and had lived in Spain for two or three years to perfect the language. Being a Quaker he was what was known as a 'non-combatant' and, because of this, many of the British prisoners were brutal to him. As a Pacifist he did not fight but he had served in the front-line helping the wounded with the Red Cross. Being a sensitive young man, the brutality and nasty remarks from some of the other prisoners made him very depressed. He suffered to such an extent that

he committed suicide by jumping from the top of the fort into the moat sixty feet below and was crushed to death. I felt so sad because he was a very nice man.

From this first fort I was then marched sixty miles south to a place called Thorn which is now called Torun, I believe. This was Stalag XXA and I was incarcerated in Fort 13. Winter was setting in and we were getting quite cold. It must have been around Christmas-time because the river was frozen.

Entrance to Fort 13, Stalag XXA, in the snow. Courtesy of Mr Paul Dainton.

Bridge and moat in snow Fort 13. Courtesy of Mr Paul Dainton.

Torun is situated in northern Poland. The capital, Warsaw, is south-east and the Port of Gdansk on the Baltic Sea is due north. It is 185 miles from the border with Germany to the west. The Germans called it Thorn though over time is has invariably been named Thoren, Torn and Thorunium. The old town was surrounded with medieval fortifications, the majority of which were demolished in the nineteenth century because they were no longer considered sufficient protection for the town.

Between 1872–94 the Prussian government built a ring of forts surrounding Torun to defend its eastern border from the Russian Empire. It thus became one of the largest fortresses in Central and Eastern Europe. Despite the expense of sixty million German gold marks, it was never besieged by Russian forces and took no significant part in the First World War either. Of the two hundred fortifications, batteries and infantry shelters, seventeen forts remained in various states of decay. During the Second World War many of the forts surrounded by dry moats were used by the Germans as prisons and Prisoner of War camps, collectively named Stalag XXA.

Over 60,000 Prisoners of War were processed through Stalag XXA over a period of five years. These included Commonwealth troops, French, Belgians, Poles, Yugoslavs, Russians, Norwegians, Americans and other nationalities. Consequently, hundreds of wooden huts were erected outside the forts to accommodate them. All but the very sick were made to work on railway and road construction, maintenance work or in building or cement works. Many were sent to stone quarries, coal mines and factories producing sugar, glass or paper.

The forts were situated both sides of the mighty Vistula River which has its source 651 miles south in the Carpathian Mountains and runs past Auschwitz (Oswiecim), Krakow, Warsaw, and Torun to the Baltic Sea at Gdansk.

It was here in Fort 13 on the south side of the River Vistula that Mr Edward Freestone was incarcerated from late 1940 until August 1943 when he was transferred to Stalag 383 in Bavaria and it was from this dank, semi-underground fort that he was sent on daily 'working parties' to undertake hard labouring tasks. At times he was 'seconded' to minor camps closer to the port of Gdansk.

Fort 4 entrance, Stalag XXA, Thorn (Torun today), Poland.

Fort 4 moat, Stalag XXA.

At these forts we were packed twenty-six prisoners to a cell. The 'beds' were made from rough wooden planks, three or four high, with about a foot to spare between each level. We just had to crawl into these with our bits of blanket or whatever we had to cover us. Here we were given 'food' but I wouldn't say it was any better – just more gruel. In those days we didn't receive Red Cross food parcels. It wasn't for about eighteen months to two years that we actually received a constant supply.

We queued up for our soup each day and ate in one big hall or just took it back to our bed if there was room to sit there. There was a table in our cell but there was not enough room for everyone to sit around it. We had a couple of slices of bread with the gruel but if you ate it all in one meal there was nothing left for the evening but if you left some it tended to get stolen, so I didn't know what to

Underground corridor, Fort 4, Stalag XXA today.

contact with civilians. When the Red Cross parcels eventually started to arrive we could take out a bar of soap and could buy almost anything with it, even a packet of tea.

We didn't hear much about what was going on outside the camp because then no-one had the means of knowing. We did hear that there was a resistance type of movement going on outside but we were never informed of what was happening. And we were so near to Chelmo, Sobibor, Magdanek, Belzec. All those places were not very far from us though we were unaware at the time.

After the Germans invaded Russia, which I now know started on the 22nd June 1941, when we were out on working parties and visiting head depots to get our materials, we used to watch the carts of bodies being pulled by hundreds of Russian prisoners. The Russians

do. I think I used to eat mine in one go and just hope for the best. Perhaps during the day I might meet a German who was a bit gullible and I might be able to bribe him to give me some bread. Out on the working parties bribing was often done because we came into

Working party from Stalag XXA Poland. Courtesy of the British Red Cross.

were by then very weak and it took dozens of men to pull a cart-load of dead bodies to a big pit they had dug. They would just chuck them in and pour lime over them, or whatever they had. Not only could we see that, but we could also smell it. The Russian Prisoners of War were treated terribly by the Germans. Of course, it wasn't so much the Russian Army that we saw but the peasants the Germans overran when they were invading Russia. Hundreds of Russian peasants and, of course, intermixed with these peasants were Russian soldiers. They were all in a pitiful state.

A lot of Polish people spoke English but there was also a sort of pidgin-type German and English used to communicate. When I was first a Prisoner of War I only knew a smattering of German but it didn't take long to pick it up because I was constantly using it to argue with the guards about different things. The only way to argue with the guards was to speak German, so I became an unofficial interpreter on the working parties.

Out on working parties we were given instructions in German such as 'Today you will lay one hundred yards of railway lines'. We would do that and work twelve hours a day. Well, we might get that done in eight hours, so the next day the guards would tell us they wanted two hundred yards of line laid today. Of course, what happened is that the men worked slower. There was always a lot of arguing going on with the Germans. There were also many Polish men undertaking slave labour.

Another of our slave labour jobs was to unload train-loads of sugar beet. We were issued with big forks and had to unload the sugar beets into silos. It was then washed and pushed into the big factory where it was made into sugar which was the raw sugar which they were famous for in that part of northern Poland. Again, the conditions under which the Germans worked us were so terrible that we had to stand and argue with them. We asked them how they could work a man if he hadn't had any food and we prisoners used to say

"Give us more food and we will work better". After twelve hours' work we were returned to the camp for a drop of soup and that was our day. We were then woken early next morning for another twelve hours of unloading sugar beet from the railway trucks. We worked six days a week and had Sundays off. A church service was arranged by the English padres who had been captured.

Underground cell in Fort 14, Stalag XXA Torun. Australians of the 26th Field Hospital Unit.

Prison Library Stalag XXA Torun. Courtesy of the British Red Cross.

Once the Red Cross parcels started to arrive more regularly we were able to have a little more food. This was a life-saver because we were becoming thin and weak. The Red Cross sent lots of books too and we were able to form a library. I then read in my cell on Sundays, and this gave me a means of escaping my predicament. I also started to write poetry.

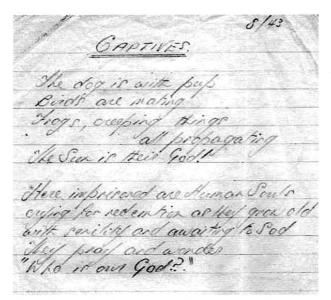

Poem 'Captives' written by Edward Freestone in Fort 13, Stalag XXA, August 1943. See right.

CAPTIVES

The dog is with pup,
Birds are mating.
Frogs, creeping things,
          All propagating.
The Sun is their God!
Here imprisoned are Human Souls
Crying for redemption as they grow old
With senility and decay, awaiting to Sod,
They pray and wonder,
Who is our God?

It was whilst I was incarcerated in a camp near Danzig that I, plus a few others, plotted our first escape. We had dug a tunnel which was discovered and we were caught. In every camp there was someone who would report you to the Germans in order to get better conditions; even the British would let you down. When the Germans discovered our tunnel we were sent to another camp which was in Bavaria. The only prisoners to be sent there were those called 'Escapees'. All the other prisoners were needed on their working parties. It was essential that the Germans kept a good work-force and they used slave labour to do it. We were often separated on the working parties. A Prisoner of War was made a friend but on the next working party he had gone, possibly even shot. You never knew.

CHAPTER FOUR
TRANSFER TO STALAG 383, HOHENFELS, BAVARIA

UNDER THE GENEVA CONVENTIONS, Articles 27–34 of the Prisoner of War Code, Officers could not be made to work unless they specifically asked for appropriate work to be found for them. Any work they did was to be paid by the detaining power, to be reimbursed at the end of War. Non-Commissioned Officers (NCOs) were to carry out only supervisory duties unless they specifically volunteered. 'Paid' work meant the prisoners received 'dockets' known as 'Lagergeld' which could be used in the camp canteens, though there was often nil to 'purchase'.

The Prisoner of War Code of the Geneva Convention was signed by forty-seven nations, though not ratified by all, in June 1929. The USSR did not attend nor sign, neither did the Japanese. Contained in this Code were ninety-seven Articles, compared with only twenty-one in the 1922 Hague Convention, and they covered every aspect of imprisonment from capture to release. No labour was to be directly connected with the prosecution of war, including transport or manufacture of arms or munitions.

The major powers of the Axis, Germany, Italy and Japan ignored these Conventions when it was convenient for them to do so, and the Soviet Union almost totally ignored them most of the time. German mistreatment of the Poles and the Russians is infamous, as is their genocide of the Jews, Gypsies and the physically and mentally impaired. Extreme maltreatment of Prisoners of War by the Japanese is also well-known. The Geneva Conventions post-war in 1949 now include Codes for the protection of civilians.

After much International pressure the Germans agreed to establish non-working Prisoner of War camps for NCOs, the first being in September 1942 called Stalag 383 at Hohenfels, Bavaria.

The Germans were wishing to be seen adhering to the Geneva Conventions at that time. The German Commandant at Hohenfels was said to be a very fair man. Stalag 383 incarcerated NCOs and a few 'Escapees' with an option to work, although most of these inmates refused. NCOs served their superiors as Batmen or did the work of Orderlies. They generally worked in an endeavour to maintain their camp, attending or teaching education, exercise, sports or artistic classes. Some worked on what were called 'fatigue parties' which included the collection from the railway station of thousands of Red Cross parcels and post and the distribution of these.

The Camp Leader was a Scot, SQMS David McKenzie, who affectionately became known as 'Old Mac'. His role was to create a cohesion based on comradeship and solidarity in the presence of the enemy, and to pool food and clothing when necessary to ensure all ranks received the same. He interviewed new prisoners and gave them advice. He also negotiated with the Germans to improve conditions and to protect prisoners from ill-treatment. In general he helped to maintain the morale of his fellow-prisoners and attended to all matters concerning prisoner welfare. In this he was assisted by others of senior rank who were called 'Men of Confidence'.

I don't know the exact mileage from Torun to Regensburg (it is 530 miles) but it took us days and days to get there. There were hundreds of us packed into one railway truck, standing up. People dropped dead where they were. We couldn't breathe, no water, nothing for days. The trouble was that there was a War going on around us. We were shunted into one section and kept there, then shunted somewhere else before

we were moved on. I believe there was an aircraft factory at Regensburg where special planes were built by the Germans. When we finally arrived we were absolutely exhausted. From Regensburg we were sent to Stalag 383 which was in a small village called Hohenfels just outside of town of Parsberg. There were 6,000 men in that camp which was mostly for Officers, NCOs, and of course, 'Escapees'.

On reaching Stalag 383 on the 12th August 1943 I felt tired, disgusted and weakened. However, because this camp had been established since September 1942 there had been good organisation with Red Cross parcels arriving regularly. Once my name was officially entered on the Red Cross list at this camp I was then entitled to receive a parcel, and one came through once a week. I was also entitled to send home a short letter of twenty-five words every month which was, of course, censored.

Letter written to his mother, 27 February 1944. See below.

Dearest Mother, I was delighted to hear you received my snap, and glad you think I look well. I am sure my mere saying "I am well" isn't quite so convincing as a little positive proof. There are men from my own Regiment included in the snap, one is my own CSM, who is a grand old boy. The second (with wrist watch) is an Oxford don, a very charming chappie. We have a lot in common. My mail from Leicester is not in abundance, although I hear they are all well, which is satisfying. Your loving son, Teddy xxx

More letters from Edward to his mother from Stalag 383, Hohenfels

Dear Mother, (19.11.1943)

I am now receiving letters direct to my new address. Mail now seems to have returned to its old regularity, which is very nice. I receive regular letters from Sybil, including three beautiful snaps. She seems to have a beautiful nature and her letters are free from all vanity. Does Willy talk of what he proposes to do after the War? I suppose Bobby will continue with his present occupation? And Myself! Well, mother dear, I should like very much to study "Art and Literature" but, of course, this requires an independent capital and possible travelling, and these chances at the moment are remote. Other than this I shall go into my own business. What do you think? As it is Sunday, a friend of mine has invited my friend and I to tea and a recital of records, which I am looking forward to. And as tunes remind us of our homes and friends I will, without a doubt, think of you. Love to all, from your devoted son, Teddy xxxx

Dear Mother, (16.3.1944)

After patiently waiting and waiting, I was today rewarded by the receipt of your charming letter of the 16th February. I have been writing a few war poems but I shall have to rewrite, or rather give them another chance, to say what I feel. Concentration is rather hard under such trying conditions, and one feels always cynical, like moralising. And I don't think I am by any means, cynical. Anyhow, I spend a joyous time listening to beautiful records. Bye the bye, it is now a year since I received a clothing parcel. I hope they haven't been lost. I am informed that you do marvellous work for the Red Cross. You were always so devotedly a philanthropist at heart. And to me always the most affectionate of Mothers. Love to you all. Look after yourself dear. Your devoted son, Eddy xxxx

Dear Mother, (3.6.1944)

Owing to a new mail system, we are now undergoing that awful unavoidable period of waiting. I presume this also affects our dear ones. However, I hope you will not unduly worry as to my welfare. I am well, with a little literature and occasional music to cheer one. Today, (as probably the date will remind you) 26 years ago you expectantly awaited the arrival of a newborn. Here I am, 26 years later, writing and reminding you of the painful, yet pleasurable incident. As to my being a dutiful and loving son, I have certain doubts, but believe me dearest, I love you and respect your beautiful soul and devotion. No love to me can be so deep as that of mine for my mother, or hers for me. Its sacredness I salute, and until I fall in love with my future wife (wherever she be) I will remain sincere to the love you have bestowed in me for women. May God grant us a speedy reunion. I am yours, as ever, a Loving Son, Teddy xxx

Dear Mother, (21.9.1944)

For four weeks I have been waiting to hear from you, yet nothing has arrived. Owing to new events, I suppose there will either be a stoppage or lull for an unknown period. However, as long as you are well, I can bear the absence of mail. Today has been extremely sad. A chappie died very suddenly and today was his funeral. Here one feels these things a little more. After four years of this awful life, to pass away, with a wife and three children, is a great misfortune. Wreaths were made from odds, and deep respects were paid by many. Do send my love to all the family. You do realise how much I desire to be with them all once more. It will be so lovely, won't it mother? Until then we must be patient, and look after ourselves. Keep well dearest, and accept all my love and misses. Your loving Son, Teddy xxx

Whilst the very harsh conditions for Edward Freestone at Fort 13, Stalag XXA at Torun in northern Poland could not have been reconciled with any spirit of the Geneva Convention, life at Hohenfels Stalag 383 in Bavaria was more tolerable. Not least, this was due to the regularity of the arrival of Red Cross food and clothing parcels as well as the World Alliance of YMCA's education and sports equipment packages. From October 1942 until October 1944 relief parcels arrived regularly and were a welcomed supplement to the German almost starvation ration. Edward Freestone found himself allocated to a small dormitory hut holding just twelve prisoners. There were larger barracks for theatrical revues, musical performances or educational activities, and space for indoor recreation and outdoor sports.

As a non-working NCO Prisoner of War camp there were certain privileges to be gained although pressure to work on the NCOs from their German captors seldom ceased. Time here could be well-spent, when not feeling too hungry or cold. This camp might well have taken the alias of 'Stalag 383 Hohenfels University of the Barbed Wire'. Prisoners were from all walks of life and many had professional and well-educated backgrounds. They willingly gave their time teaching and organising a great variety of educational classes, musical pursuits, theatrical performances and sporting activities.

Edward Freestone acted as stage staff and took part in several theatrical performances. He was in the audience of many musical events both classical and popular, he read many books, attended educational classes, groups and sporting activities. He also took lessons in German and Spanish and wrote poetry.

Almost one hundred 'clubs' were formed and many prisoners were members of six or seven, such as the 'London Club', the 'St Andrew's Society', the 'Sussex Club', the 'Aussie or Kiwis Clubs', the 'Welsh Club'. Much was learnt at the 'Talks and Debates Circle'. At their meetings refreshments were served, perhaps Ovaltine and

Poem 'Battlefield' written by Edward Freestone, January 1944. See right.

BATTLEFIELD

Beautiful green,
This bloody grass.
Comrade – quite unseen,
Rest your Head,
>*Sleep, let the dead*
>*March past.*
The river freely
Flowing here
Shall tell his Mother,
She'll shed a tear.
'Never (have) another'
And in solemn silence bear,
The growing old,
The silvering hair,
For a day to come
When she will meet –
>*Her unforgotten Son.*

'To Bert in gratitude for many pleasant hours spent in forgetting the horribleness of War.

In memory of seeing one of my Army friends mown down by machine gunfire on La Bassée Canal in 1940, lying in the beautiful grass in France'.

Kreigie-made cake and even home-brewed hooch. Some featured a cabaret show whilst others ran football tournaments. They organised quizzes, talks, spelling competitions and much more – all for a weekly subscription of one cigarette! The 'Freemasons' Club', banned by Nazi Germany, secretly met behind bolted doors! By the end of the War there were eighty-two 'Brothers' from many nationalities.

Ultimately, Stalag 383 had a well-stocked library of thousands of books and many men studied to equip themselves of a profession or trade to benefit themselves for when the

Drama Group Stalag 383. Costumes by Edward Freestone (pictured top left).

Stage Staff, Drama Group, Stalag 383. Edward Freestone in shorts.

'great day' of their release arrived, their optimism of an Allied victory never faltering throughout their captivity. Subjects such as advanced French or three grades of Spanish were taught. Regular requests were sent via the Red Cross for equipment, books, material and text books for educational classes and study groups. Some men were spending nearly all day in educating or re-educating themselves. Rather than brooding on hardships this gave them value in their future, and study had hugely restorative effects.

Within this multitude of subjects many men sat RSA (Royal Society of Arts) and Matriculation Exams. Out of two thousand candidates there was a 90% pass, the work being processed by the International Committee of the Red Cross in Geneva.

At its height of activity the curriculum comprised of eighty-four different subjects from Aeronautics to Zoology, dozens of languages, Engineering, Bee-keeping, Hairdressing, Carpentry, Town Planning to Psychology. Many men just read for pleasure in appalling discomfort, freezing conditions and with pangs of hunger. This quote by Euripides certainly rang true:

"Even in words there is pleasure when they bring forgetfulness to present woes".

After several months at Stalag 383 I chummed up with a Scottish fellow called Norman Drummond and we became friends. His father was a big whisky manufacturer in Glasgow although Norman was a male secretary who wrote shorthand, which was unusual I thought. He was a clever man who spoke good German. His education had been much superior to mine. I was an 'elementary' schoolboy and he was a 'college' boy!

Mr Norman Andrew Drummond was born on 22 November 1916 at La Chatelaine, Milngavie near Glasgow. His parents were Andrew Bauchop Drummond, a ship owner, and Annie Byars

Drummond. Norman had one half-sister and their address at the time of his enlistment in August 1939 was 11 Crown Terrace, Hyndland, Glasgow. Not unusually for that era, Norman was trained as a shorthand-writer and it was that skill that enabled him to record verbatim the BBC News received on the secreted crystal radio sets, then later transcribe this information for the illicit camp 'Newsletter'.

When Norman joined the 172/58th LAA Regiment, Royal Artillery, which later became part of the BEF (British Expeditionary Force) for the Invasion of France in May 1940 he was given the NCO rank of BQMS (Battalion Quartermaster Sergeant). It was whilst retreating after these landings in June 1940 that he was captured by a German soldier on the end of Calais Pier, the soldier damaging Norman's teeth with the but of his gun.

Norman was then transported or marched as a Prisoner of War to Stalag XXA at Torun in Northern Poland. In August 1940 he was sent to Stalag XXB at Marienburg (Marburg) for a few months and then back to Torun by November 1940, where he remained undertaking hard labour until May 1943. All this time he was in charge of working parties where he continually undertook sabotage of a small kind, this largely being on German vehicles.

In May 1943 Norman was transferred to the NCO camp, Stalag 383 in Hohenfels in Bavaria. Thus Norman Drummond, as well as Edward Freestone, serendipitously avoided the forced march west from Torun to Germany towards the end of the War, a march on which so many prisoners perished in the harsh Polish weather.

Norman and I decided to 'muster' together by sharing our food parcels. On opening a food parcel it was tempting to eat it all in one go but when two of us shared our parcels the food went further. When we cooked, we cooked for two.

For just over two years Red Cross parcels arrived weekly at Stalag 383 at Hofenfels, most being sent from Britain or Canada by sea in one of eight

Norman Drummond and Edward Freestone, Stalag 383.

specifically marked Red Cross ships to Lisbon in Portugal or Marseilles in France. They were then transported by rail to collection points of the International Committee of the Red Cross in Geneva, Switzerland. Distribution to the camps was by rail or truck. They were financed by the Allied Central Prisoner of War Committee, the British or Commonwealth Red Cross Societies, and the Order of St John of Jerusalem, and were packed by their volunteers. In addition, one parcel a month or quarter was supplied and packed by kindly mothers, devoted wives or other members of a prisoner's family. These cardboard boxes measured around ten inches by seven inches and five inches deep, were up to eleven pounds in weight and were tied with string. A box might contain –

A small tin of bully-beef (corned beef), small tins of meat roll, herrings, sardines, processed cheese, margarine or butter, vegetables, condensed or powdered milk, a packet of biscuits, five ounces of chocolate, small jar of jam or marmalade, a small packet of prunes or raisins, coffee or cocoa, quarter pound of tea, four ounces of sugar, egg powder, a little salt, pepper, a small bar of soap, shaving equipment. Fifty cigarettes or flake pipe tobacco was sent separately.

They might also contain small surprises like some boiled sweets or pancake mixture, a pair of hand-knitted gloves, a balaclava hat or a small towel.

Red Cross parcel store, Geneva, Second World War. Courtesy of the British Red Cross.

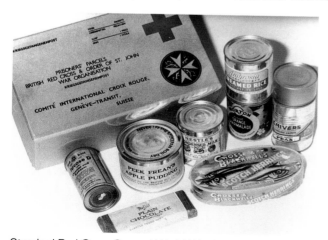

Standard Red Cross Second World War food parcel contents. Courtesy of the British Red Cross.

Prisoners would form hut syndicates and appoint a quartermaster and a cook because the pooling of ingredients meant, for example, the production of something resembling a pie or stew. Sometimes just two or three kindred spirits 'mucked in', taking it in turns to act as cook or bottle-washer. When the number of parcels was inadequate prisoners were compelled to share the contents of one Red Cross parcel between two or three, sometimes more.

Other types of parcels delivered through the International Red Cross were First Aid Safety Kits to medic POWs and packages of books, games, educational material, drama requirements, and sporting equipment. Most of the latter was supplied by The World Alliance of YMCAs, The International Bureau of Education, The Ecumenical Commission for Assistance to POWs, The European Student Relief Fund, The International Federation of Library Associations, The Advisory Committee on Reading Matters for Prisoners, and the Swiss Catholic Mission for POWs.

The receipt of these necessary though inadequate supplies contributed directly to the survival of most Allied Prisoners of War and importantly increased their morale. In addition, without the constant negotiations forced by the International Red Cross Committee on the German Authorities, in a bid to persuade them to adhere to the Geneva Conventions as well as to allow camp inspections, many thousands of POWs would certainly have perished and many certainly did when these Conventions were ignored.

Prisoners' Red Cross food was supplemented by 'German rations'. Under the Geneva Conventions the captors were supposed to feed their prisoners on the same standards as their home-based troops. However, since most German troops were not 'home-based' their own rations were often depleted, especially as the War progressed. It was due to these circumstances that the POWs were able to bribe their guards with the temptations of certain contents from their Red Cross parcels. The purchasing

Red Cross food parcels being received at Stalag 383. Courtesy of the British Red Cross.

power of British and American cigarettes on the German black market was considerable.

The German rations for prisoners consisted of one-fifth of a stale, dark rye loaf and usually a cup of watery soup per day; the 'soup of the day' being either sauerkraut, dried vegetable, cattle food, swede and birdseed, fish-head, or cabbage and worm. On a good day the soup might contain barley, potatoes, animal fat or horse-meat.

Some prisoners at Hofenfels were known to have cooked hedgehogs and rabbits, the latter species being bred by inmates for their meat but also for their skins which could be used for making gloves or slippers. However, their rabbits were often confiscated by the German guards who ultimately put a stop to the breeding.

We even had radios in the camp. We made our own crystal sets using bits of wire wrapped very tightly around a pencil then used drawing pins stuck into little bits of wood, with razor blades to make a condenser. The only thing we had to buy, or bribe the guards for, was the crystal itself and the headphones, but once we got that we were in contact and could get the BBC News. That was how we got our news and we were even fortunate enough to have enough cigarettes to buy what they called a 'people's radio' which had two valves in one and had been commissioned by Hitler to be available to all 'his people'. For about 2,000 cigarettes we could buy one, but the problem was hiding it, so we used to hide it inside our gramophone which was in a special case.

Another interesting thing was that we produced a 'News Sheet' – sometimes hundreds of copies a day, giving information about camp life, education classes and activities but also news of the War. We melted down the jellies sent in the Red Cross parcels and laid them flat on a try. When almost dry we wrote the news using an indelible pencil. We then placed the sheet of paper on this jelly,

POW group at Stalag 383, Edward Freestone wearing cravat, third from right, back row.

pressed hard and lifted it off. For the preparation of the news my friend Norman, being a stenographer, took down any news from the radio in shorthand then transcribed it onto the sheet in indelible pencil. When we got news from the BBC we knew it was correct, at least, as far as we were concerned it was!

CHAPTER FIVE
ESCAPE

AFTER ALMOST FOUR YEARS of being confined Norman and I couldn't stand any more so we decided to plan some sort of escape. Other men had tried it but had been caught. Stalag 383 was said to be a camp that no-one could escape from, and when they did, they never got far before being captured.

The reason escapers or 'gallopers' as they were called never got far from Stalag 383 was due to the fact that it was located within the south-eastern region of one of the most important and extensive Bavarian Military Training Areas of Germany – Grafenwoehr and Hohenfels.

The Training Area was initially established by the Royal Bavarian Army in 1908, extended over 19.5 square kilometres, and had its Headquarters close-by at Nuernberg (Nuremberg). Bavarian combat troops during the First World War, 1914–18, numbered up to 550,000 soldiers. Two-hundred thousand of these lost their lives in that terrible War. In 1919 the Bavarian Army was integrated into Germany's 100,000 man force, a number limited by the Treaty of Versailles. However, when the National Socialist Party came to power in 1933, led by Adolf Hitler, a massive military build-up began with the introduction of the general draft in 1935. By 1939, in contravention of the Treaty of Versailles, the small 100,000 German Army had increased to 3,000,000, and by 1944 to 9,000,000 soldiers. Grafenwoehr was expanded to the west by 350,360 acres and throughout the Second World War the Training Area served as an activation base for new units. The Area was visited by both Hitler and Mussolini.

Being almost a part of this Training Area, with its extensive German military activity, meant that a successful escape from Hohenfels Stalag 383 without recapture was almost impossible.

The first escape we tried was by just walking away from a 'fatigue party' whilst our guards weren't looking. We planned to walk the two hundred miles south of Parsberg to get to the Swiss border. We did this without advice and help from the Escape Committee, of whom, at the time we knew little. Whilst we did almost reach Switzerland, exhausted and hungry, we were caught whilst trying to cross the boarder and the guards there returned us to Stalag 383.

Corporal Michael McCallen RASC (late King's Regiment) was covertly known as the 'Scarlet Pimpernel of Hofenfels'. As one of the 'Men of Confidence' he lived a life of constant scheming, dangerous action and high suspense in organising the 'Escape Committee'. He did this with the help of several other talented Officers and returned Escapees and for which, after the War, he was awarded the BEM for his services.

'Mac', as he was known, took part in dangerous tunnelling and wire-cutting at night whilst avoiding sweeping searchlights. He organised the creation of escape equipment, kit, maps, civilian clothing and the acquisition of rations and German currency. He also arranged classes on the 'philosophy of escaping' for the 'escape minded' and drilled them on health and the practical matters of 'galloping'.

Mac's 'Kreigie' (prisoner) helpers were masters at map-making, compass making, tailoring, cobbling, and producing documents and photographs. He was also assisted by artists, wood carvers and ex-forgers, and he frequently used his talent for bribing guards and others in the acquisition of a myriad of components for the creation of a necessary implement for escape.

All these accoutrements for escape had to be hidden from the German guards which was not an easy task since they often carried out searches of the huts to the extent of taking up floorboards and rifling through the prisoners' sparse possessions. Much was hidden in the larger plywood boxes which had held Canadian Red Cross parcels. They were then lowered into huge cavities dug into the ground. Some were even hidden in the latrines or the cookhouse.

Becoming an escapee or 'galloper' required great courage. There were German posters displayed around the camp stating:

Escaping is a Damned Dangerous Sport!

Stay in the Stalag where you will be safe

Otherwise you will certainly lose your life.

Eventually Norman and I decided that if we were to make a successful escape we would need to get right away from the camp quickly – which meant by train. We knew that Parsberg Railway Station was about ten miles away and we came up with the idea of escaping by train to Vienna and setting up some sort of escape route. We thought that two young men, even in disguise, walking along would be picked up by the Germans. Most German young men were at War or in uniform. There were only disabled and old men to be seen. Our first idea was to escape both dressed as women, but eventually we devised a plan to travel as husband and wife, Norman being disguised as a Danish professor. I was to be his 'wife'.

With the assistance of the 'Escape Committee' in our preparations it took us nine months to organise our plan. In Stalag 383 there were some very clever prisoners. They had been professionals. One of them had been a teacher at Vienna University and he drew up all our papers as he knew exactly what they would have looked like. He wrote out in official lettering 'Doctor so-and-so' travelling from Copenhagen University to the University of Vienna, studying veterinary science and especially tuberculosis in cows for the Wehrmacht, and travelling with his wife' – it was all officially stamped.

Many members of the Escape Committee committed nine months of careful preparation and planning for one of Stalag 383's best-planned escapes. Norman Drummond spoke German fairly well and Edward Freestone's German was adequate, although both were schooled to speak it with a Danish accent. By studying maps they were drilled in the geography of Vienna and were taught the correct behaviour in German civilian conversation coached by a one-time native of Vienna, Irvine Poppa, and now a Prisoner of War from Palestine. Norman acquired the requisite impressive professional manner, whilst Eddie was trained to walk in ladies shoes and assume the gait of a female. He was also trained to manage a female hair style, make-up and clothing, and taught to acquire the gestures of a woman.

The Red Cross had sent equipment to assist our studying. This included some T-squares for geometrical drawings and these were made from very hard wood which could be utilised by being cut into different official stamps. A genius in the camp called Bill Jones could engrave different types of stamps. His eyes were so unusual that he could write minutely, say within a letter T. He used to send back messages to England in his Red Cross letters. To anybody else these included a letter T, but actually comprised a message which would eventually end up in an Intelligence Department. A man called Charlie Kober wrote the Gothic type perfectly and composed letters of introduction. There were ordinary German civilians working in the camp doing repairs. Their passports were whipped whilst they were working and much of that documentation was copied by this man, aided by Geordie Nicol and a Sergeant McDougall.

The real difficulty he had was faking the passport paper. The paper we had was white, and passport paper used in those days was a buff colour. To overcome this he used magnesium crystals diluted in water in which he soaked the white paper. A prisoner must have bribed a guard to get the magnesium.

Once soaked in this solution the white paper became beige, and when dry looked the exact colour of a passport. Lovely passport paper was made and inscribed to look very official with the addition of the stamps made from the T-squares. It was very official-looking, so much so that our passports passed five Gestapo inspections.

As for the photographs, these were again taken with the help of some contents from the Red Cross parcels. We could buy anything from the Germans. They were very poor and had nothing to live for really. They lived on coffee, black bread and sauerkraut. They'd sell their souls for a few cigarettes and, of course, with a few cigarettes we could buy a camera and films. In one of the big huts in the camp some ingenious fellow had dug a very deep hole about six feet by six feet under the floorboards and draped the inside with blankets. We sat in that little hole and our passport photographs were taken.

Norman Drummond passport photo, dressed as Professor for the escape.

Our escape 'attire' was not only provided by the Escape Committee. We had befriended a lovely Polish girl called Anastasia Evanski who lived outside the camp, but did slave labour within the camp kitchen, and she offered to help. Although she had been a 'college girl' one of her jobs in the kitchen was to peel the potatoes for most of the day for the German guards.

Edward Freestone passport photo, dressed as wife, for the escape.

Anastasia Evanski, Polish college girl who carried out slave labour for the Germans in the kitchens of Stalag 383.

We were allowed to go to the cook-house in the mornings to get hot water to make our tea. Many cauldrons of water were boiled to service thousands of men. One morning a German guard suggested to us that for a few cigarettes we could become 'intimate' with this Polish girl. Some women were 'intimate' with the prisoners, even with German officers' wives. It was possible and it did happen, not in the camp but outside – just for a bar of soap. Norman and I told the German that if this was his German 'culture' he could keep it! Anastasia really appreciated our honourable reply. The next morning we found a note by the tap thanking us for our kindness. We left a note in reply and we set up a correspondence and sometimes left her chocolate, coffee or soap. We became very friendly and learnt a bit about what was going on outside the camp.

For our escape Anastasia supplied me with the type of clothing I needed, such as ladies' shoes, stockings, make-up and handbag. I had naturally curly hair which I grew for nine months and about which I got nasty remarks from other prisoners suggesting that I was 'queer', but I passed these off by stating that I was preparing to appear in a new camp play. The prisoner tailors in the camp had to get to work on my clothes, making them look feminine. Harry Morgan and Stan Hawkins made a suit for Norman using Red Cross blankets, and German civilians or guards were bribed to obtain men's shoes, a tie, shirt and nice suitcases.

The 'Escape Committee' consisted of a couple of Officers and four or five other prisoners – men who had tried to escape before could be included because they knew the circumstances and they wouldn't let you down, but the Officers were in charge and they finalised the details. They were all very secretive about what they did because there were so many informers in the camp.

Sacks of mail for POWs , International Committee of the Red Cross store, Geneva. Courtesy of the British Red Cross.

One of the regular jobs Norman and I did after being driven by truck to Parsberg Railway Station was to unload parcels and mail. With 6,000 men in the camp, mostly receiving one parcel a week and one letter a month, there was a lot of unloading to be done. Civilian boys and girls who were around at the station were as friendly as they dared be but were afraid. Back at the camp, a chore for other prisoners was to repack the sacks with any straw and string not needed from the emptied Red Cross boxes. They then had to stack these sacks onto large trucks which were driven by the guards to a big shed just outside the gates to await refuse collection. Sometimes these sacks were carried by the prisoners.

Norman and I watched this going on for several weeks before we decided that this was going to be our way out – in one of those sacks of Red Cross rubbish! Our plan was to get to Vienna and then into Hungary, over the Balkans, into Syria and meet up with the Allies.

We set a date for our escape – the 20th April 1944. Our civilian clothing was packed into our suitcases together with my make-up, handbag and a small supply of food. The night before we were due to escape the Officers from the Escape Committee approached us and told us we were expected to undertake some 'intelligence' work and send back information on bombing raids, bridges, transport and train movements in Vienna. Norman was to write postcards in a German sort of code which were to be posted to a German, obviously bribed, to be passed into the camp to the Escape Committee who would then relay it to an Intelligence Department in England.

To assist the first stage of our escape there were, thankfully, two strong prisoners in the Red Cross depot, and once we were inside our sacks and the suitcases safely in another sack, these men threw us onto a lorry. Sacks were randomly pierced by German guards using their bayonets before being transported outside the camp gate, but luckily we avoided any 'piercing'.

Once outside we were again 'thrown' into the big shed to await a refuse collection and the doors of the shed were locked. As soon as dusk came we climbed out of our sacks and found the specially marked sack containing our suitcases. We then waited until dark before climbing up big beams to get into a little ceiling. We then silently opened the skylight and climbed out onto the shed roof.

We had to wait for the search-lights from the German machine gun posts to swing to another area before we could lower ourselves down and inch our way across the field to the woods. On our bellies we moved, then lay low, moved and then lay low, and it took us about four hours to get to the woods. As soon as daylight came we changed into our civilian clothes and started to walk.

Although we had eaten some dried apricots, pears and apple and some rolled oats, we had no water, so Norman suggested we call at a little house along the road. The occupants were reticent but friendly. Norman told them he was a German soldier returning from leave and that his 'wife' was pregnant and needed water. I didn't speak at all. Norman spoke such excellent German that they actually believed what he told them. Having a Scottish accent meant that his German sounded rather northern, and with so much movement going on in Germany a person could come from anywhere.

We rested in a wood and waited until it was dark and then walked for most of the night, arriving at Parsberg Station at six o'clock. We knew there was a train due in at seven. My 'husband' bought two tickets and was not recognised by any of the locals who had often been around when we collected the Red Cross parcels and mail.

Once on the train our problems seemed to begin. We were asked by Gestapo soldiers for our papers and passports but everything was accepted as in order. I can't remember the name we used on those documents. By this time my face was getting a bit bristly but even with no water in the train toilet and

Parsberg Station near Hohenfels, today.

house. We were used to being without food, having almost starved for four years, so a bar of chocolate lasted us a day. In our suitcase we had cigarettes and soap and other things we could use for bartering. In my little vanity case handbag I carried my 'feminine' needs. Of course, we also had German currency.

Originally, our intention was to get out of Germany quickly but because we were told by the Escape Committee that information was needed back in England, we just had to stay awhile to observe. What we sent back was probably minute but it might have been a little piece of the jigsaw in the puzzle which the Allies were looking for.

having to spit on my shaving brush before I could use my razor, I powdered my face and put on lipstick, and came out of the toilet looking refreshed! Keith Gadd, the Australian Prisoner of War hairdresser at the camp had made my hair look very feminine and nothing unruly had happened to it. I had even been trained to walk like a female.

We arrived at Regensburg Station and had to change trains to the Vienna Express, for which Norman bought us first class tickets. After several more Gestapo passport checks, and burying our heads in German newspapers, often standing in a train corridor, we arrived at a main station in Vienna. We boarded a tram and after a short journey got off and went into a cinema where we felt safe watching a film. We then walked around observing what was happening. We found a lot of bomb damage, low morale amongst the people, and general disillusionment with the War. The Allied bombing raids were beginning to take their toll. There was the 'thousand planes' raid whilst we were there but we had to just keep walking the streets. We couldn't stay in one place. We were avoiding the bombs and the Germans as well!

We bought extra postcards to add to what we already had and Norman wrote them in German code and sent them off. We walked around for several days and slept wherever we could, not daring to approach a boarding

CHAPTER SIX
CAPTURE

AFTER ALMOST A WEEK of living in such bad conditions, and dressed as a woman, I couldn't go on much longer. We therefore felt it was time to make a 'contact' at an address which had been given to us by the Escape Committee which was in the Donau Canal area. I spruced myself up and we went to find the café rest-house on Hollandstrasse. We had been told to go to number twenty-two but there was no building there so we decided to go to number seventeen opposite which was a café. The proprietor, who appeared to be if anything a Jew, looked as if he might be the man we wanted.

Danube Canal near Hollandstrasse in Vienna, today.

After a walk around we again returned to the cafe, sat down and Norman ordered some coffee and rolls. When these arrived Norman dropped some hints that we were two refugees trying to get out of Vienna. The proprietor said he would speak to his wife and everything looked well, his wife suggesting we might be able to spend the night, but I think he went away and phoned the Police whilst his wife kept us talking. In no time an armoured car and an open truck arrived carrying Gestapo and German police. I said to Norman "I think

we've had it" and he replied "Yes, I think we have". And we had!

Author outside café in Hollandstrasse, Vienna.

Three plain-clothes Gestapo came storming in, revolvers at the ready, demanding that we put our hands up. German policemen guarded outside. They suggested we were espionage agents but we said we were escaped Prisoners of War. They argued that as I was a woman I could not be. I put my hand into my blouse to try to retrieve my 'falsies' to prove I was a man but they thought I was going for a gun and fired shots into the air. They then handcuffed us and marched us through the streets to a nearby Police Station where we were locked up in separate cells for the night, our hands cuffed behind our backs.

Author inside the café.

Early next morning we were taken to the main Gestapo Headquarters, known as the infamous Vienna Zuchthaus, where we were beaten almost unconscious by the guards using the buts of their rifles. We were then taken to a room with white walls where we were chained and hung from big hooks and made to walk down sloping boards beneath us to ensure we were suspended off the wooden platform. We were given no food nor water and left hanging for twenty-four hours with chains gripping our wrists. Our bodies were numb by the time they started to interrogate us.

We had been trained by the Escape Committee just what to say in the eventuality of being caught and interrogated. We regretted that we had not had time to destroy our forged papers. A Gestapo paper specialist examined them minutely before he convinced himself that they were not genuine. He repeatedly accused us of having stolen them. Norman and I were separated for the first part of our interrogation and they told each of us that the other had confessed to espionage and that a firing squad was standing by for the one who didn't confess. They marched us into a bare yard but we just stuck to our

rehearsed story of being escaped Prisoners of War and demanded we be treated within the Geneva Conventions. But they didn't care, for that seemed to mean nothing to them.

We were then taken to a block of cells which were sectioned by iron bars and told we were 'political prisoners'. In our cell there were twenty-six other prisoners of many nationalities. This included an Austrian boy who had happened to say he thought the Germans would not win the War. We had to share just twenty flea-ridden blankets and there was a little bucket in the corner for us all to do our 'business'. In the next two sections there were women almost naked, crying and in a severe state. I realise now they were Jews awaiting deportation and death. Strangely, prisoners in the male section were not naked. Our only food was an 'extermination diet'. We could talk or shout to those who spoke German, Italian or English. We were the only English prisoners.

After a few days the Chief of these Gestapo sent for us and in his room he had our suitcases. Funnily enough they never opened those damned things – all the chocolates, cigarettes and soap inside! We had the keys in our pockets which they could have taken, or they could have just slashed the cases open. The Gestapo Chief spoke to us in English and said he was sorry and didn't want to see us treated like this. Norman and I were a bit surprised. He said he had been a waiter on the Hull-to-Hamburg lines before the War and knew English people and liked them very much. We asked him what he was going to do and told him what our suitcases contained. He was delighted and accepted everything we gave him. We insisted we were escaped Prisoners of War and that he had responsibilities under the Geneva Conventions to return us to our camp Stalag 383. Perhaps it was because the Germans were by now losing the War that this appeared to frighten him and he said he would see what he could do. When Stalag 383 was first contacted they said that no-one was missing from the camp – a

Memorial at the infamous Vienna Zuchthaus, Gestapo HQ on Morzinplatz. The building was destroyed by Allied bombing. It was not excavated but laid to lawn. It is the graveyard of many.

tribute to the 'cover up' system on roll calls. However, our fingerprints were then sent and the Commandant at Hohenfels had to admit that we had indeed flown from his cage.

We were eventually called to the Gestapo Chief's office and told we were going back to our camp. Three guards accompanied us on the trains and, once back, we were actually received with cheers from our fellow prisoners. They were so glad we hadn't been shot and the Officers were pleased we had sent some information on the postcards. No-one had escaped from Stalag 383 and got so far before. From then on Norman and I we were given the nick-name of "The Two Viennas".

We had to appear before the Camp Commandant who demanded to know just how we escaped. He suggested we could not have done so without the help of a German. There again we held out and did not divulge our method of escape. As punishment we were put into solitary confinement in small cells for a month.

On release from the 'cooler' back into the main camp Norman and I were placed in a specially guarded hut. One of these guards was the Deputy Commandant, a squat little man with a Japanese look whom we nicknamed 'Moto'. He was a vicious man. In the past we had seen him shoot a man who couldn't jump up from his bunk and stand to attention because he was sick. Moto used to shout at us "Raus, raus, you two Viennas" each morning. One evening he marched Norman and I outside and down the side of our hut away from the search-light beams. He then took a loaf of bread from his jacket and gave it to us stating he admired our escape and provided we could give him a few cigarettes, soap or chocolate, he could

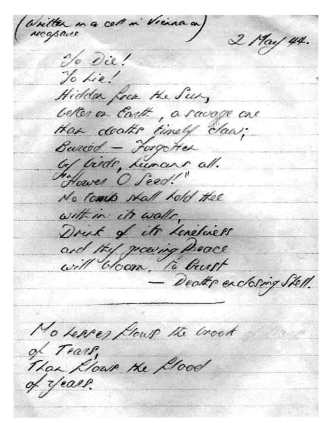

Poem 'Soul Imprisoned' by Edward Freestone written in solitary confinement after capture. See right.

Soul Imprisoned

To Die!
To Lie!
Hidden from the Sun,
Better on Earth, a savage one
Than death's timely claw.
Buried — Forgotten
By birds, Humans, all.
Flower oh Seed!
No tomb shall hold thee
Within its walls.
Drink of its Loneliness
And thy growing Peace
Will bloom to burst
— Death's enclosing Shell.

No lesser flows the brook
of Tears,
Than flows the flood
of Years.

bring us more bread. He came to us with bread regularly after that and told us that if we were thinking of escaping again we should let him know and he would come with us! He told us he had been on the Russian front and what he saw up there frightened him so much that he wanted to get out of Germany. This man, who had brutally frightened everyone and made the prisoners' lives hell now wanted 'safe conduct' from the camp because he thought the Germans were going to lose the War!

The autumn and winter of 1944, and spring of 1945, were terrible times of starvation because Red Cross parcels almost stopped arriving, and we were not supplied with fuel for fires. The Germans were putting all their efforts into fighting the Allies. We knew the War was going pretty badly for the Germans and felt sure the Allies would soon be victorious.

CHAPTER SEVEN
THE END OF THE WAR

FOR MANY ALLIED PRISONERS of War the period between November 1944 and March 1945 – their last winter in captivity, was their worst. The Allied Invasion from the West, and Russian invasion from the East, led to chaos in Germany. Allied planes were bombing towns and cities, destroying buildings, railways and roads – all routes for the transportation of Red Cross relief.

As in most camps, Red Cross parcels failed to arrive at Hohenfels for six months. Consequently, the men were forced to rely for sustenance on the German rations. By March 1945 these were down to eight hundred calories a day. Prisoners were becoming weakened by starvation, collapsing at roll calls and hibernating in their bunks. Although the stoppage of Red Cross parcels was due to disruption of rail and road, it was also due to plundering by German troops in retaliation for the Allied successes. Even fuel for warmth was withheld, so the bitter cold chilled the prisoners' bones. Added to this was extensive overcrowding due to the arrival of ever more prisoners, most being transferred from camps closer to the Russian advance.

It was not until 22 March, one month before liberation, that Red Cross parcels arrived at Hohenfels, enough for one parcel between two. By liberation on 22 April 1945 the men had not recovered from their weakness, emaciation and near-starvation.

One day, I think it was the 17th April 1945, all the prisoners were ordered to evacuate the camp. We were told this march was to the south of the Danube. Norman and I didn't want to do that. We decided to crawl into one of the empty rooms, climbed up the chimney breast, and remained there until the camp was evacuated. Apart from those in the hospital wing,

I believe we were two of only a handful of prisoners to hide and avoid this march. Before their march the Germans mowed the buildings with machine-gun fire but our luck held out because the bullets failed to reach the inside of the chimney breast.

At liberation one thousand five hundred prisoners were found in the camp hospital, several dozen had decided to hide then walk, but over five thousand were forced-marched south to Regensburg, although were thereafter liberated by the Allies.

We remained inside the chimney breast for about twenty-four hours. When we felt it was safe we moved down, and after gathering some scraps of food, we just walked out of the open gate. We had heard the rumours of the advance of the American and British forces, so for three days we just walked towards the Nuremberg area where we knew General Patten was heading. We had enough food because we were used to surviving on almost nothing. Food was not important. We just walked and walked.

Eventually we could hear heavy firing but as we walked through villages we saw no German soldiers, just civilians. Ourselves, and others who were walking, were all ignored. The battle for Nuremberg was fierce. General Patten's troops were giving it a heavy bashing. When we eventually met with American soldiers they were surprised at how badly we looked and they guided us to the outskirts of Nuremberg to Furth airfield, I think it was called, where they were flying in supplies.

It is difficult to describe how I felt meeting up with the Americans. It really was the most important thing in my life. I just lay on the grass, looked up at the sky and thought how lucky I was to be there.

In mid-April 1945 the 3rd American Army, commanded by General George S Patton, moved into the Eastern Bavarian area with 100,000 troops. The four Military Training Areas of Bavaria, which included Grafenwoehr and Hohenfels, were soon occupied and put under US Administration.

Immediately after the collapse of the War many former Prisoner of War camps were used to hold German prisoners, camp guards, SS troops and other defeated enemies. They were later utilised as 'Displaced Persons' and Refugee 'Holding Centres'.

Following Hitler's suicide and Germany's surrender, the whole of Germany was divided into four occupied zones by the USA, the Soviet Union, Great Britain and France, although unfortunately, in 1947, due to the differences between the Soviet Union with the other three victorious powers, the Western and Eastern Blocks were formed. These differences encompassed political, military, ideological and economic issues and resulted in 1949 in the division of Germany into the Federal Republic of Germany and the Russian-led German Democratic Republic.

This 'Cold War' with Russia necessitated the military training of the other Allied powers within the Federal Republic of Germany. On 4 April 1949 the North Atlantic Treaty Organisation (NATO) was formed to provide a collective defence. The Bavarian Military Training Areas therefore became of strategic importance. The whole Area became not only an exclusive location for gunnery training but also a training centre for modern communications, tactics and command exercises for the NATO Armed Forces.

What is left of Stalag 383 at Hohenfels today appears as a small field within the massive Joint Multinational Readiness and Simulation Centre. In 2005 it was renamed the Joint Multinational Training Command. It is one of the most important commands of the US Army in Europe and continues to train Forces of more than forty Nations. This includes Germany which was reunified in 1990, after the collapse of Soviet Russia, to become the Federal Republic of Germany.

Stalag 383 Hohenfels today. Author with Mr Norbert Wittl, Public Relations Officer of Joint Multinational Training Command, Hohenfels, Bavaria.

After several days on the outskirts of this airfield and being pushed further forward by other arriving masses, a big aircraft landed which looked rather important. When the steps were lowered who should walk down but General Patten himself! He walked towards us and stayed to talk. He seemed a nice man and said he could see that we had suffered. He realised there would be no fighting from the area we had just left and felt he could advance as fast as he liked.

After an hour he told us to walk down the road a little way to be treated to some coffee and dough-nuts. We went to this little mobile canteen and who should serve and talk to us but Marlene Dietrich herself! I was quite thrilled about that.

The fate of Stalag XXA in Poland – In January 1945, with the Russian troops advancing, the Germans forced-marched the prisoners of Stalag XXA west into Germany during a Polish winter in which temperatures dropped to below zero. Many thousands died from hypothermia, starvation and exhaustion. The Russians liberated the prisoners left in the camp hospital on 21 January 1945.

Today Fort 13 and its surroundings are still in use and occupied by the Polish Armed Forces. Many of the other forts are derelict but on the northern perimeter of the old town Fort 4 is open to the public. Despite having a café and being available to hire for functions, this semi-submerged, dry-moat brick building appears dark, dank, cold and foreboding.

During the course of my research I fortuitously met Mr Paul Dainton, an Undertaker who lives in Leigh, Lancashire. His father was Lance-Corporal Thomas (Tom) Dainton of the Royal Army Service Corps, 1939–45. As part of the British Expeditionary Force he landed in France where he was captured by the Germans in May 1940. For the duration of the War he became a Prisoner of War in Fort 13, Stalag XXA, Torun. During this time he endured much hardship. The final part of his captivity included the horrendous forced march in sub-zero temperatures from Poland into Germany. Many of his fellow Prisoners of War died on this forced march.

Tom Dainton died in December 2001 aged almost 91. He had said very little to his family about his experiences as a Prisoner of War. One of Tom's sons, Paul, had an interest in Military History and became an enthusiast, collecting war medals and memorabilia. This lead him to become curious about what really happened to his father during the War. Consequently, in September 2007, together with his wife Sheila, Paul made a pilgrimage to Torun.

In Torun Paul and Sheila fortunately met a very helpful taxi driver called Hennryk Sadowski who facilitated a meeting with Major Mariana Roshinsky. He commanded the Fort 13 building which is now part of an important Polish Army base surrounding the actual fort. Paul and Sheila found their 'tour' very emotional, for the interior of the fort had been left almost as it was when the prisoners were forced to evacuate in early 1945. On a wall of a developing 'museum' there was even a group black and white photograph featuring Paul's father!

From 1939 until 1945 as many as 60,000 Prisoners of War of many nationalities passed through the forts of Stalag XXA, 20,000 British through Fort 13 alone. The idea came to Paul Dainton that there should be some sort of Memorial erected to commemorate this. Once back in Britain Paul organised a campaign for donations to achieve this. In the Polish harsh weather of January 2009 Paul, together with seven others, returned to Torun taking with them a cheque which included donations from the Wigan, St Helens and District branch of the Grenadier Guards. For the Fort 13 'museum' they also took a display of British Army badges, buttons and other memorabilia. Sheila's cousin, Eric Radcliffe, aged 84, laid a poppy wreath at the temporary Memorial. Eric had served in the Tank Regiment at the D-Day Landings of 1944.

Mr Paul Dainton with brother, Harry, at temporary Memorial Stone, Stalag XXA, Fort 13, 2009. Courtesy of Mr Paul Dainton.

By the spring of 2010 the Polish Army had organised the initial memorial stone to be split, polished and engraved by Polish masons. The Memorial stone was laid by British and Polish Forces. In English and Polish it reads:

Memorial erected by funds raised by Mr Paul Dainton to commemorate all British Prisoners of War held at Fort 13, Stalag XXA during 1940–1945. Courtesy of Mr Paul Dainton.

In memory of all British Prisoners of War

Held at Stalag XXA Thorn – Fort XIII

1940–1945

Paul, his family and colleagues were invited by Major Mariana Roshinsky to the Polish Liberation and Remembrance Day Parade on 11 November 2010. Wearing his father's War medals Paul marched through Torun with the Polish Army and visited the Memorial in Stalag XXA, Fort 13. This was a poignant moment for them all. Throughout their visits to Torun they have loyally been assisted by the taxi driver, Hennryk Sadowski and his family who have also invited them into their home for Polish feasts. Paul has written an account of his father's experience in Torun, which includes brief memoirs of some other Prisoners of War held there, and he frequently gives talks to interested groups.

The medieval old town of Torun on the northern bank of the River Vistula is the birthplace of the Astronomer Nicolaus Copernicus (1473–1543). In 1997 it was designated a UNESCO World Heritage Site because of its original Gothic brick buildings, monumental churches and town hall. Torun escaped substantial destruction in the Second World War but sadly Mr Edward Freestone, Mr Norman Drummond, and many thousands of others, never saw its beauty. Today, the old town and riverside are illuminated at night creating an impressive atmosphere which draws many tourists. In 2007 the old town of Torun was added to the list of the Seven Wonders of Poland.

Copernicus, Torun and the River Vistula today.

CHAPTER EIGHT
RETURN TO ENGLAND

AFTER THREE OR FOUR days waiting at Furth Aerodrome some Dakota aeroplanes landed with supplies and we were then able to board for a flight to Brussels where we were placed in a Red Cross Centre. As we walked into its main hall the Warsaw Concerto was being played and to me that sounded very lovely. After two weeks of Red Cross attention we were eventually flown to an airfield near Guildford – after five years as a prisoner I was home! I was back in my green and pleasant land. I really did enjoy that. I thought how pleasant it was to see trees shorter than the German and Polish trees. The low-lying oak trees and beautiful greenery impressed me very much.

Near Guildford we were placed into transit camps, examined for illnesses, and given endurance tests. We were then put on trains and granted six months' leave. Norman was sent to his home in Glasgow and I made my way to Southampton where I met my mother at home at 1 Surrey Road, Woolston which luckily had not suffered bomb-damage. My mother was delighted. We had such a nice family reunion.

Although I had been passed as medically fit, mentally I wasn't quite right. I became very nervous and didn't like to sit or talk in company. I'd sweat and have to move away. As a Prisoner of War I had virtually lived on top of others but as a civilian it took me longer than a year or so to rehabilitate myself. I even felt claustrophobic in the presence of a nice young friend, Sybil, who had written to me throughout the War and who came to meet me on my return.

I spent my time doing a lot of reading and walking. I received a small back-pay from the Army and I had to spend it all on my keep whilst recuperating. I was too ill to work. I went to my doctor, to an Army doctor, and to the British Legion for advice but really got none. In the end I gave up hope of getting any help. I spent a fortnight in Glasgow staying with Norman. We had a nice time but after that we lost touch – he went his way, working – and I went mine. Our civilian lives were so different.

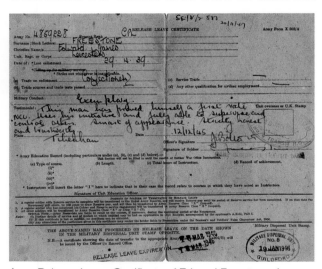

Army Release Leave Certificate of Edward Freestone, January 1946. Exemplary, first rate NCO, uses initiative, fully able to supervise, smart, strictly honest and trustworthy.

The Queens Hotel, Helensburgh, Scotland.

After the War Norman Drummond returned to the family home in Glasgow. In 1950 he married Kathleen Coventon and in 1952 they had a son named Norman Scott Drummond who became a Chartered Accountant. Sadly, he died prematurely in 1992 aged just forty. In 1975 Norman married Marion Ross (nee Wallace). Professionally, he became a Hotel Manager, first in Inverness and then in Helensburgh where, from 1950 until his retirement, he ran The Queens Hotel. During the 1990s until his death in 2006, Mr Drummond was the loving partner of Mrs Phyllis MacGregor.

Mr Norman Drummond died in March 2006 aged 89 years, an unsung National Hero.

Norman Drummond with Phyllis MacGregor, Scotland. May 2005. Courtesy of Phyllis MacGregor.

In the Summer of 1946 I met a man who had owned W R Price's bakery shops in Southampton before the War. He was having trouble with profitability and asked me to come to sort things out, which I did. This bakery made a lot of steak and kidney pies, sausage rolls and so on. After the meat was cooked I saved the residual fat and used that to cook more pastry. A lot of other chefs didn't do that. Rationing of food was very strict, it being so soon after the War, but the extra pastry made with this fat resulted in greater profits for the shop. I then got work at James' Electric Bakeries in Victoria Road. On an extra high tide, and with heavy rain, the water from the River Itchen nearby would flood the underground kitchen and we had to work standing in water up to our ankles!

Wages were low at this time but I was living with my mother and that helped finances for both of us. My Grandma Tappin had died in 1937. In early 1939 my mother had actually re-married to a man called Samuel Simpson Johnson who, like my father, had been born in the North East, though he had grown up in Woolston. He was a younger bachelor but they formed a good relationship and they found work together at the Royal Motor Yacht Club in Sandbanks, Bournemouth, where he was the Motor Launch Driver and my mother followed her sons into catering, becoming the Assistant Cook. They had a nice life working at this Club until the War changed all that. Sadly, in early January 1945, when they were back living at 1 Surrey Road, Woolston, he died from leukaemia, so my mother was alone again.

A little later my younger brother, Bob, also came back to live with us because he was going through a divorce. We went everywhere together, including the Sun Hotel pub in Weston Lane, where we often had a glass of wine whilst talking about our Wartime experiences with its owner, Frank Gilley, who had been a Prisoner of War in the Far East. Of course, we got on famously, though I never made any lady friends. I lived with my mother until I was thirty-seven.

Eddie (now called Ted) Freestone with his younger brother Bob, late 1940s, Southampton.

In 1954 I went to work for a Mr Hallam in his Lowford Bakery which was in a delightful little village outside Woolston. When I started there the shop was taking £150 a week but when I left, fifteen years later, the weekly takings were £2,000 and with five vans on the road – that was what I enjoyed doing – building up a business. Just after the War, as a 'Returned Prisoner of War' there was a Southampton Council scheme offering sponsorship for small businesses to start up. I did enquire but what I was offered wasn't enough, and I didn't wish to take a loan because I never liked owing people money, so I missed out on the opportunity to run my own business.

One of my responsibilities as a Manager was to take on staff and one young lady I employed was Joyce Best, known as Joy. We struck up a relationship and ended up marrying in 1955. I was thirty-seven though she was younger. We rented number 11 Surrey Road in Woolston and had a daughter, Kim and a son, Neil. In our time there they attended St Mark's School. We eventually moved to live above Lowford Bakery and my wife worked alongside me. We had two more children, a daughter, Sharon and a son, Simon, who both went on to attend the lovely Lowford village school. We also had another child, Lindsey but sadly he died aged just four months. That was very sad for all of us.

Mrs Joy Freestone, 1950s.

I was earning around £21 a week with £5 deducted for our rent. Besides the routine baking I produced lovely birthday and wedding cakes. However, in 1969 the owner of Lowford Bakery sold out to one of the large conglomerates for £60,000 – a lot of money then – and the bakery was replaced by a business selling fish and chips. That was not the sort of cooking I wanted to be involved in, so I got a job at the large Mullard's electrical components factory in central Southampton. We obviously had to leave the 'tied' accommodation at Lowford so we were homeless. It took us five months to secure a rental on a Council house, during which time we were split up, with Joy and two of the children staying with my sister, and the other two children and I staying with relatives elsewhere. Our move to Sholing was not my choice but we're quite happy now.

I spent almost another fifteen years working at Mullard's in their canteen. Lovely people worked there and I was very happy.

Edward Freestone on left with wife Joy and children, Kim, Sharon, Simon and Neil. Uncle Will on right, c1969.

Each day I cooked bread rolls, scones, buns and gateaux for up to three thousand staff – morning coffee, lunches and afternoon teas. One day a manager asked me to make a birthday cake for him and after that I made dozens for other staff, including wedding cakes to order, and I made quite a profit for the canteen.

At the time of the Queen's Jubilee in 1977 the Duke of Kent visited our factory and I was asked to produce a commemorative cake. I did some research and decorated the cake in the Duke's Regimental colours. I was very well-known in Mullard's. Almost once a month I featured in their staff magazine called 'Contact' and I produced confectionery for some famous people. In 1982 I received advice from a Mullard's staff accountant to retire at sixty-four rather than sixty-five. I really would have liked to have stayed on. I now occasionally help a friend in his bakery because I love to be creative.

Looking back at the time I wrote poetry as a Prisoner of War I think that stemmed from a desire to express myself or to explode. I would have liked to have written stories or done something artistic and original but I had to remain as a Confectioner in order to earn money to live on. I feel there's a lot to be said for appreciating what you have in life and be happy. After the experience of being a Prisoner of War for five years I've never worried about eating a lot of food. To me it's just a means of fuel. I'd like to see the world a bit more equally balanced with the Third World having enough to eat. We also need to educate to prevent over-population.

Edward Freestone, Master Baker at work, Southampton, 1970s.

Mr Edward Freestone, Master Confectioner.

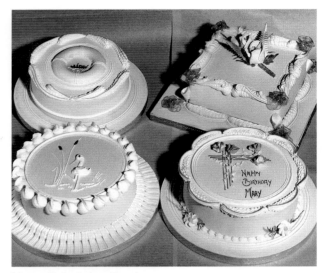

Master Baker's handiwork.

and to visit the part of Germany where I was imprisoned. Also Vienna – I could take you to the exact location of the café where Norman and I were arrested by the Gestapo. I can see it now in my mind's eye.

It would be nice to go to Scotland to find Norman Drummond or to trace Anastasia Evanski and her brother, Eugene, who actually came to see me at the very end of the War. During the War he had been in France and before returning to Poland, he came to England to visit friends and actually came to see me to thank me for helping his sister in Stalag 383. Anastasia was romantically involved with one of my prisoner friends and I think he really loved her. However, he felt loyal to the girlfriend he left behind who was faithful to him all through the War so he felt obliged to marry her on his return. I suppose that's one of the laws of War.

I'd like to go back to Leicester to see what's happened to the place in which I was so happy working and experiencing 'culture',

Mullard's staff and Master Baker, *Silver Jubilee* cake, 1977.

I would have loved to have painted, written or even sung. I admire beautiful singers. I suppose in my own way I've been artistic. Some of the cakes I've produced have given a lot of pleasure to a lot of people. I would have liked to have done something original, though you tell me my story actually is!

Mr Edward James Freestone died on 7 January 1991 aged 72 years

A talented and gentle man.

Escapee of Stalag 383

and Graduate of Hohenfel's University of the Barbed Wire.

An unsung National Hero.

Wedding cake by Edward Freestone.

Mr Edward Freestone, Christmas 1987 with his father's watch awarded 1910 for being an expert local football trainer.

THE COALBROOKDALE TO CZECH CONNECTION

CHAPTER ONE
THE LIFE OF MR ARTHUR VINCENT ASTON-NICHOLAS, 1858–1942 THE COALBROOKDALE CONNECTION

IN THE VILLAGE OF Coalbrookdale, Madeley, Shropshire, an area of great Quaker influence, Arthur Vincent Aston was born on 23 October 1858 to twenty year old Hannah Aston. In that same year Hannah married Arthur's father, Alfred Nicholas, who was a year her senior. They were betrothed in the Parish Church of Coalbrookdale on 15 December. Henceforth, Arthur was given the surname of Nicholas although much later in his life he would adopt the use of both surnames and be known as Arthur Vincent Aston-Nicholas. Alfred worked in an iron foundry. His father, William Nicholas, was a moulder in the same industry where Hannah's father, Vincent Aston, also worked as an iron fitter.

Holy Trinity Church, 1859. The village of Coalbrookdale is in the background.

By 1861 Arthur's father had escaped the manual hardship of the foundry to become the keeper of the Hand and Tankard Inn on Workhouse Road, Broseley, Wenlock. This was close to the area of his birth but situated on the other side of the River Severn. Arthur now had a brother called William who was four months old. Ten years later, according to the 1871 Census, the family were again living in Coalbrookdale. It appears the family were living with Hannah's widowed father, Vincent Aston. At this time Arthur was almost thirteen and William was ten.

Coalbrookdale and Broseley are places of great significance in the history of iron ore smelting since they were areas where coke could be easily hewn from drift mines in the sides of the valley. It was in this place it was first discovered that 'coking coal' burned in furnaces at the optimum temperature to produce iron of a superior quality. With these resources close-by the world's first cast-iron bridge across the River Severn, linking Coalbrookdale with Broseley, was built in 1778, its location named Ironbridge. The world's first wrought iron was also produced in this small area, which was the birthplace of the Industrial Revolution, a 'revolution' that was a major turning point in history and the most important event in the evolution of humanity since the domestication of animals and the development of agriculture. It transformed Great Britain and the world. In addition, the quality of the clay in Broseley was unparalleled, leading to the manufacture of impeccable earthenware and porcelain.

By the 1850s a number of British exports were beginning to wane because British pattern-designers were ill-equipped to produce new concepts or fashions. France and Germany had respectively set up state-funded art and trade schools and were providing their industries with designers of such superior talents that their products were flooding the British markets. Consequently, the British Government realised that state funding for training of craftsmen and designers was urgently needed if it was to combat the foreign competition. Accordingly, the Department of Science and Practical Arts was established. Its base was at the National Art Training School in South Kensington. 'Art workmen' or 'design ornamentalists' (not easel painters) were trained under what became known as the South Kensington System. This establishment was to become the precursor to the Royal College of Art. Apart from the students, many pupil-teachers attended to gain extra qualifications, notably the Art Master's Certificates. There were also five National Scholarships and annual grants of fifty pounds for two-year courses.

In 1852 the tile manufacturing business of George and Arthur Maw, Maw and Company, relocated from Worcester to Benthall Works at Broseley although it was not until five years later that it became profitable. By 1860 encaustic decorative floor and wall tiles became the height of fashion. They were made by a technique that burnt in the colours. Hand painted and transfer tiles were produced. Some were gilt with the entire design executed in gold. These beautiful tiles were very much desired for the floors and walls of entrances, fireplaces, bathrooms, orangeries and gardens of the grand houses of the Victorian era. Even the Alhambra Palace in Grenada and Maharajas' palaces in India were decorated with tiles from Maw and Company. These ceramic tiles were also hygienic and hardwearing. Consequently, they were supplied for hospitals, schools, shop interiors, churches, ships and public baths. Maw and Company became the most important and largest tile manufacturer in the world.

Decorative tiles, Severn House, Coalbrookdale. The home of Arthur Maw and family prior to 1907 when it was purchased by the famous Engineer, Scientist, Inventor and Liberal, Thomas Parker. It is now The Valley Hotel.

Literary and Scientific Institution, which became the Coalbrookdale School of Art.

Many of the employees of Maw and Company were trained at the Coalbrookdale School of Art which Arthur Nicholas and his younger brother, William, both attended. This school of art, with its roots as the Coalbrookdale Literary and Scientific Institution and its base now in South Kensington, was set up by the Government initiative following the London Great Exhibition of 1851. Grants were given to suitable or gifted schoolchildren, and to apprentices, to enable them to attend part-time as pupil-teachers, mostly in the evenings. The majority of these students were from poor families, as were Arthur and William.

1875 by Arthur Nicholas

1876 by Arthur Nicholas

Arthur Nicholas was employed by Maw and Company. Indentured apprenticeships were readily available and Arthur had considerable artistic talents. Below are examples of two plates he painted for his family in 1875 and 1876 at the ages of just seventeen and eighteen respectively. His name, date, and 'Maw & Co' are on the reverse.

In 1878 Arthur was awarded one of the five, two-year, National Scholarships at the National Art Training School in South Kensington. This achievement meant he had won national competitions and medals. Major changes for the Nicholas family lay ahead. With his parents, Alfred and Hannah, his maternal maiden aunt, Annie Aston, and his grandfather, Vincent Aston aged eighty, Arthur relocated to Chelsea. Since his scholarship was for limited sessions, we can assume he also taught at local schools. By 1881, at the age of twenty-three, Arthur's profession was an 'Artist'. His father, Alfred retrained to become a cabinet maker; such were the opportunities for developing skills at the time.

At the National Art Training School Arthur received some of the best art teaching then available in Britain, much of it based on practical demonstration. Italian Renaissance was the style being promoted. He was taught by the school's Principal, Edward J Poynter, Alphonse Legros, Jules Dalou and Edouard Lanteri, though his main teacher was Francis Wollaston Moody. Between the mid 1870s to 1880s the most influential of the Victorian classical painters, Sir Frederick Leighton, RA, was commissioned by South Kensington Museum (now the Victoria and Albert Museum) to produce two large lunette (crescent-shaped) mural paintings at either end of the south court of the museum. One is called 'The Arts of the Industry as Applied to Peace' and the other, 'The Arts of the Industry as Applied to War'. In this massive undertaking he was assisted with under-painting, panels and decorative borders, by Francis Moody and a group of his students. Overall supervision was given by Edward Poynter. There is a record of regular payments having been paid to Moody and his students. Below is an eighteen inch square painting of a detail from the 'The Arts as Applied to Peace' mural by A A Nicholas, dated to 1885, which today hangs in the National Museum of Scotland in Edinburgh.

Meanwhile, Arthur's younger brother William remained in Shropshire where he was employed as a pottery painter. On the 1881 Census

he was living as a 'boarder' with a family in Ironbridge and was continuing his part-time studies at Coalbrookdale School of Art where he won the Bronze Medal prize that year. Technical subjects were also taught there which included Machine Construction and Engineering Drawing, Practical Mathematics, Magnetism, Electricity and Applied Mechanics. Not surprisingly,

Detail from 'The Arts of the Industry as Applied to Peace' painted by A A Nicholas, 1885. After Sir Frederick Leighton RA. Courtesy of the National Museum of Scotland, Edinburgh.

William later became a Mechanical Engineer. In 1896, aged thirty-five, he was an Engineer living in Chelsea and had married a school teacher called Jessie Worman, the daughter of a railway stationmaster from Hertford. By 1901 they had three children, Bertram, Elsie and Jessie, but America was beckoning offering great opportunities. Mrs Jessie Nicholas, together with her three children, sailed from Southampton to New York on the ship 'St Paul' on 5 July 1902. William was there to meet them. The couple had three more children in New York whom they named Arthur, Doris and Vivian. Later the family moved to Fairfield, Connecticut where William ran his own very profitable mechanical and steam engineering tool-making business. They had a long and successful life.

It was in London that Arthur met Frances Henry Newbery (1855–1946). Newbery, like Nicholas, came from a humble background. Born in Devon, he grew up in Bridport, Dorset, where he became an art teacher. In 1875 he moved to teach in London and attended the National Art Training School as an evening student to improve his qualifications. In 1881 Frances Newbery resigned his school teaching posts to become a full-time Art-Master-in-Training at the National Art Training School. Although the details are not known, it can be assumed that Arthur Nicholas did likewise. He was talented enough to win awards and medals similar to those gained by Frances Newbery.

By 1885 the need for industrial artists was being felt in Scotland. Consequently, the giant industrial city of Glasgow extended its school of art under the auspices of the South Kensington System. Accordingly, the man who had by now acquired both artistic prowess and leadership qualities, Frances Henry Newbery, was appointed Headmaster of this establishment. He was just thirty years of age. He obviously recognised the abilities of his colleague, Arthur Vincent Aston Nicholas, for he appointed this man as the first dedicated Design Master.

Arthur was twenty-seven years of age. It was no mean feat that these two men, both from modest backgrounds, had risen to such accomplished positions.

As Design Master at Glasgow School of Art, Arthur became particularly focused on teaching design from flower and plant form and at times conducted his classes at Glasgow's Botanic Gardens. He became a familiar figure, often walking the school's corridors carrying a flower. In 1892 he specified that he wished to teach 'the figure as applied to Majolica, book illustration, mural decoration' and so on. He also had much experience in stencil work, underglaze painting, enamels and lustre work. He taught students from all social classes, students who were full-time, part-time and industrial apprentices. Amongst other accomplished pupils, Arthur taught the now world-famous Charles Rennie Mackintosh, Margaret and Frances Macdonald, Herbert McNair and other major Designers who went on to produce the 'Glasgow Style'.

Frances Henry Newbery, known as 'Fra', was Headmaster and then Director of the Glasgow School of Art from 1885 until his retirement in 1917. On his appointment he organised the teaching to be the most up-to-date and in line with the needs of Glasgow's manufacturing community. At the same time he made it interesting and adapted to individual students' needs. Working students attended in the early morning or evenings, whilst mostly middle class ladies studied during the day. He employed only staff he considered to be 'artist teachers' and invited leading modern designers such as William Morris, Walter Crane and Lewis F Day to lecture. This resulted in great improvements in the artistic environment and examination performance. By 1897 Glasgow School of Art had become the most successful in Britain and attracted staff of international standing. The school became independent of the South Kensington System when the Scottish Education Department was formed in 1901. At this time Frances Henry Newbery, together with his teaching professors, established a four-year Curriculum leading to the new qualification of Diploma, a qualification unaltered until 1979 when Degrees were introduced. Francis Newbery was a highly accomplished networker and gifted publicist. He rubbed shoulders with the rich, the poor or famous, be they artist, craft or industrial designer, actor, architect or writer. He encouraged students to develop their own style and individuality and promoted their work both here and overseas.

During thirty-six years of teaching at the Glasgow School of Art, from 1885 until 1921, Arthur Vincent Aston-Nicholas, as he became known, held various posts, from Design Master to Assistant Professor, or Joint Professor. He taught in the Departments of Design and Decorative Art, Drawing and Painting, Plaster Modelling, or Textiles and Wallpapers. He was also a Member of the Committee for Assessment of Diplomas, Travelling and Maintenance Scholarships, and Bursaries, and for three years a Staff Council Member. His initial salary of £150 a year varied depending on the number of sessions he taught. By the time of retirement he was earning over £225 a year, a significant sum in 1921. In the twilight years of Arthur's teaching he was affectionately referred to as 'Old Nick'.

Arthur Vincent Aston-Nicholas never married. His ageing widowed mother and Aunt Anne Aston were both resident with him in Glasgow on the 1901 Census and his brother, William, visited them there from New York in the summer of 1910. By 1911 Arthur was a boarder in the house of a widow and her two daughters at 9 West Princes Street, Glasgow. His mother and aunt had returned to London. His brother, William and wife, Jessie, with some or all of their six children, visited Great Britain in 1905, 1910, 1914 and 1915. At the start of the First World War Arthur and William were fifty-six and fifty-three respectively. Consequently, they were above the age to join active service. Their mother, Hannah and Aunt Anne both died in 1916 at 68

Park Road, Bushey, Hertfordshire and are buried in Stanmore Cemetery. Arthur was present at the death of his Aunt Anne. At the time he was living at 17 Arlington Street, Glasgow West. He had travelled south to be at her bedside. In her Will she left all her worldly goods of eighty-six pounds, seventeen shillings and three pence to her nephew, Arthur.

In 1917 the very able Frances Henry Newbery, together with his wife Jessie Rowat Newbery, who was famous for Art Needlework, retired to the south coast of England to Corfe Castle, Dorset, where Frances continued to paint. By this time their two daughters, Margaret and Mary, were both married to artists; Margaret to William Douglas Lang and Mary to Alexander Riddle Sturrock. Prior to retirement Fra Newbery developed a debilitating depressive illness made worse by the news of the death of colleagues and students in the First World War and this illness recurred in 1932. He died at Corfe Castle in 1946 aged ninety-one. There are paintings by Frances Henry Newbery hanging today in the Town Hall of Bridport, the little town near to Corfe Castle, where he grew up from the age of three.

At some stage after retirement in 1921, Arthur Vincent Aston-Nicholas also chose to live on the south coast, perhaps for the more clement weather of Bournemouth and to be near his life-long famous colleague, Fra Newbery. In his youth he was known to have been one of 'Newbery's great friends'. They were colleagues for almost forty years. It is not known if their close friendship endured, but for ten years from 1920 Fra Newbery often took the train to Bournemouth on Fridays in order to attend concerts at the Winter Gardens. Whether he met with Arthur to attend these concerts, it is not known. Sadly, nothing is known about Arthur's experiences after his retirement in 1921.

Nineteen years passed before the advent of the Second World War brought documented change to the life of the talented, elderly bachelor, Arthur Vincent Aston-Nicholas.

CHAPTER TWO
THE EARLY LIFE OF ANNA ERIKA JENNOVA
THE CZECH CONNECTION

I WAS BORN ANNA Erika Jennova on the 8th May 1930 at 74 Rudolfov, a small village in south west Czechoslovakia which is very close to a town called Ceské Budëjovice. My father's name was Frantisek Jenne. He had been born in this same house in 1886 at a time when the country was part of the Austro-Hungarian Empire. Frantisek was my father's Czech name and Franz was the German version. The surname of Jenne was the male name, whilst females of the family were called Jennova. I believe the 'ova' is also added for females in other countries such as Poland and Slovenia.

My mother, Marie, born in 1905, had the maiden surname of Fischbäckova, pronounced Fischböckova, and her mother's maiden name was Gutschkova. These were German families from a place called Mugrau which is in the Bohemian Forest in the county of Horice. Mugrau is around thirty miles from Rudolfov. My mother had an older brother called Joseph and younger siblings called Anna, Henry and Elfrieda. I believe the Fischbäcks moved for work to Rudolfov after the First World War. As a child I used to visit Mugrau by train with my mother in the summer holidays. I remember my Auntie Matilda who must have been my

Marriage of Marie Fischbäckova and Frantisek Jenne, 1927 with his children Klara, Mitzi, Franz and Karl.

mother's aunt. She had two daughters and a son in their twenties. The family lived on a very big farm surrounded by fields and woods. I used to love going there because I was allowed to help with milking the cows and drank fresh warm milk. We never drank cows milk at home, just goat's milk.

My father was widowed twice before he married my mother in 1927. By his first wife he had children Klara, Mitzi and Franz and by his second wife, who died in childbirth, a son, Karel, whom we called Karl. Karl was six years old when my father married my mother. She was twenty-two and he was forty-one. My brother, Valtr, whom we called Walter, was born in 1928, though my sister, Helene, whom we called Helli, wasn't born until 1945 when I was fifteen, so it was just Walter and I brought up together. By then Klara, Mitzi and Franz had left home; Klara to train as a dressmaker, Mitzi to do a secretarial course and Franz to train as a hairdresser. Karl was cared for on a shared basis by one of his mother's sisters who had no children whom we called Auntie Schwartz.

We were always led to believe that my father was an only child though in the past five or six years we have discovered that he had a much younger sister named Marie who was the person who lived next door to us. We knew Marie as 'Auntie Marie' and she was married to a man whom we called 'Mr Prochaska' who was a Sales Rep. They had two children, Rudolph and Antonia, whom we called Rudi and Toni, and they were our great friends. At the time I didn't know they were my cousins. Our house and their house had once been just one house but when my father's parents died the house was split between my father and his much younger sister, Marie, as we now know. My mother was very friendly with 'Auntie Marie' but my father never spoke to her nor her husband. There must have been some family rift, though we don't know the details. Mr Prochaska was a very nationalistic Czechoslovakian and was politically active. Perhaps that was the reason.

In his youth, my father was trained to be a cabinet-maker, at which he was very skilled. When commissioned to make furniture he would live at the customers' home until his work was completed. However, he either enlisted or was conscripted into the Austro-Hungarian Army Hussars for a while where he worked with white horses, so I suppose that was the Cavalry. The state of Czechoslovakia was not formed until 1918–19 after the First World War. On his return, and as time went by, the need for his skills waned and died because a lot of furniture was being made by machinery in factories. He therefore took on a job at Ceské Budĕjovice railway station and by the time I was born in 1930 he had worked his way up to become Station Master in charge of Freight. He had a navy blue uniform with red epaulets and a cap with red braid and red lettering.

Frantisek Jenne, Austro-Hungarian Hussars, c.1906.

Marie Fischbäckova back left, Westen Enamel Factory staff, near Ceské Budëjovice, 1922.

Before her marriage my mother worked at the Westen Enamel Factory which was just outside Ceské Budëjovice. She knew my father because he lived next-door-but-one and she probably cared for his children from time to time before and after he became a widower in 1921.

I remember the day when my aunt came rushing into our house to tell my mother that their mother, Magdalena Fischbäckova, who lived two doors away from us, had just died. I used to visit her a lot to play with her dog. She was a widow with grown-up children and seemed a lonely lady. She was always working in the garden, about the house and in the fields. She died in 1935 so I would have been five years old. After that my memories are of starting kindergarten in the local village, fighting with my brother Walter who was two years older than me, and of going to school aged six. I had several friends of around the same age as me who lived close-by. I remember the lake outside my house with the avenue of trees either side – Linden trees in fact, which were especially lovely in

Anna Erika and Walter, 1935.

summer-time when in blossom — they had a beautiful smell. We used to swim in the lake in summer and skate on the ice in winter. We put our skates on inside our house, walked across the snow and slid down onto the ice. Those are my first memories.

We had very cold winters and warm-to-hot summers. Snow was always guaranteed and on some occasions it was piled high to the guttering of the houses. Sometimes we would go to school on skis or by sledge because the snow was so deep. If it was icy we used to skate to school.

Walter, right, and friend 1940. Skiing to school.

The village of Rudolfov was rather spread out. There was one prominent building which we called an old castle because it had crenellated walls. It was only ever used for functions such as Council meetings, important parties or upper class wedding receptions.

As far as I remember, our house was rendered white and it had a pattern in a yellow relief around the window-frames. The interior walls were painted with a type of torque mix on which my father would make patterns with a special comb or stencils. The house had three bedrooms and looked like a house with rooms upstairs but it was just a hayloft in those days where my father kept his workbench and carpentry tools. The entrance to the house was through the gate on the right-hand side. Our only inside water tap was in the tiled entrance lobby where there was also a chest of drawers lined with zinc. Amongst other things, my mother used to store flour there and golden sugar which came in cone-shaped lumps. Many a time I would pinch some by using the special little hammer to knock a bit off. The kitchen was on the left and there was a bedroom on the right from where access could be gained to the third bedroom, which had no windows, and access to the cellar. In the kitchen there was a big old cooker similar to an Aga and opposite that was a work table with a bed behind it in which my mother and father always slept. The kitchen flooring was linoleum though on the wooden bedroom floors we had one or two rugs. On the other side of the kitchen, which was always the cosiest room, was a big table and a corner seating arrangement by the window at the front of the house with the view of the lake and the lovely avenue of trees.

There was an old credenza next to the kitchen table — I believe it's called a sideboard these days. There was also a door to the second bedroom in which were a set of double beds piled high with duvets. My father's writing desk was also in there. No-one, except him, was allowed to use it. This room, which was once Walter and Karl's bedroom, was only used when we had visitors or at Christmas-time.

The house had a very big garden. In fact, it was a three-layered garden. The lower part was for vegetables, the next layer was for gooseberries, redcurrants, blackcurrants, blueberries, cranberries or mushrooms. Another step up and there was the orchard with apples trees, plum trees and pear trees. There was an old bench on a patch of grass under a cherry tree. My father used to cut the grass with a scythe – there was no such thing as a lawn-mower in those days. We had every possible fruit, which made us independent. My parents loved their garden and my father in particular spent most of his free time there.

The lake and the avenue of trees in front of No 74 Rudolfov.

Marie and Frantisek Jenne with Auntie Wittek at top of back garden of 74 Rudolfov, 1934.

Oil painting of 74 Rudolfov, nineteenth century. Artist unknown.

74 Rudolfov today.

We also owned fields on the other side of the village where my father grew potatoes, wheat or rye. He was also able to produce straw for the pig, sometimes a cow, rabbits, and goats, of course. I loved helping to harvest the potatoes because my father would make a bonfire and cook some potatoes with their skins on in the hot ashes, though not in tin foil as we might today. That was a lovely lunch – an enamel cup full of goat's milk with hot potatoes to burn your mouth and hands!

We usually kept a pig in an old shed at the back of the house, as well as goats. We had our own smoke-house. Smoked pig or goat was very nice. We kept chickens too, so there was always a supply of eggs or chicken meat, and there were rabbits in cages, two of which my brother Walter and I cared for. I didn't mind eating rabbit for Sunday dinner provided it wasn't my rabbit which was killed. Every time we had rabbit I would run outside to see if mine was missing! I preferred it when my father shot rabbits in his fields.

I remember my mother did a lot of baking. In the summertime, when our stove wasn't on, she would make bread, cakes and buns then take them to the local bakers to have them cooked in their ovens. She also took plums to dry on top of their ovens which produced prunes. Dumplings were very popular. My mother made them with a mashed boiled potato and flour mix, plus an egg and a little milk. After steaming the pastry patties she would pour over a little melted butter or fat, or whatever was in the household at the time. She also made fruit dumplings which were my favourite food, especially when served with a type of custard or just breadcrumbs, ground sugar or melted butter.

We made our own sauerkraut with the cabbages my father grew. Mother would slice huge cabbage heads very thinly and place them in a barrel in three or four inch layers. She would then add a layer of salt, then sliced cabbage again, and so on, until the layers came over half way up the barrel. Walter and I, with bare feet, would then tread down these layers so that more layers could be applied. By that time in her life my mother wasn't very keen on getting into the barrel herself. When the barrel was full she would add a few sliced apples and cover with a board then wheel it on a little buggy into the cellar which was on the same level. Once it was there she would cover the lid with heavy stones and leave it to ferment. Cabbage is not sour until it has been fermented and sauerkraut has no vinegar nor fluids in it whatsoever. The salt draws fluid out of the cabbage. There were no onions in it, though they were added, together with caraway seeds, apples and a little sugar when we warmed it, if that was wanted. It had a crispy but soft texture.

The washing was done in the outhouse at the top of the garden which was a separate building with its own boiler, water supply and washing drum. There was a wash-board on which to rub the washing clean. The washing drum also served as a bath-tub for our weekly baths. The youngest child would bathe first and the water used for the next. Dad would be the very last! The only toilet we had was outside next to this wash-house. When it was very cold in winter we were allowed to use a 'goes-under' bed pan inside the house.

We had a very idyllic sort of life. Nothing really to shout about, but it was happy. We never wanted for anything and were self-sufficient. We had enough warm clothes because nothing was ever thrown away. It was only my father who had a suit bought, rather than home-made. The clothes in the wardrobes and in the big trunks were probably over a hundred years old. I used to dress up in some of these though many were re-modelled for us by a dress-maker who would come to our house and stay for a week or longer. We would feed her and she would become part of our family over that time. I used to love the lady who came. She taught me how to sew and that stood me in good stead for what was to happen in my future life.

Also living within our household was a lovely old lady we called Auntie Wittek, a widow who had no children whom I believe was a great aunt of my father. She helped with the general housework and chores or did a bit of crochet or knitting. She slept in that dark, little bedroom with no windows — that was her room. During the War Auntie Wittek became a little senile but she remained living with us until her death in the summer of 1945.

My father had a newspaper every day in the German language. Saturdays was a special day because a novel, usually historical, was published in instalments. We weren't allowed to touch the paper until my father had seen it and cut out the relevant pages. After a few weeks the novel would be complete and my father would then have it beautifully bound into a book. I remember we had 'Catherine the Great', 'Napoleon', 'Anna Karenina' and others. I wish we still had those books. Perhaps someone still has them now.

We had a radio which was about the size of the cooker. I can't remember listening to music though. It seemed it was switched on just for news. I was encouraged to leave the room when it was on during the War. I was protected by my parents from any bad 'goings-on'. Eventually, during the War, all radios were confiscated by the German soldiers just in case anyone was listening to foreign stations.

At the age of six I went to the village school which I attended for six years. There were just over forty pupils and all ages were in one classroom — a couple of rows for the youngest, then more rows for the next age-group and the next. We had just one or two teachers. I didn't really like school and if I could get away with doing as little as possible, I would. We were taught in both German and Czech. We would learn a subject in German for one week and then we would go through the same subject in Czech for the next week. Eventually, we were asked questions in one language and had to answer in the other. It was not difficult to become properly bilingual because we were living in a bilingual village. Living on the border, we were a mixed society or group — half German, half Czech — if anything, my family was more German than Czech. Most of the more rural villages were totally Czech.

Anna Erika Jennova, centre front row (smallest), 1936. Walter, back row far right. Kindergarten or primary school, Rudolfov.

I was brought up a Roman Catholic but now lapsed. We went to church every Sunday with my mother though Walter and I had to sit in one of the front two pews where all the children sat. My father never went to church except to attend funerals or weddings. He didn't believe in it. In fact, for a short time I attended a Roman Catholic school. In 1942 when I was twelve I left Rudolfov village school to attend the senior school which was in Ceské Budějovice. However, I was at this school for less than two years when it was damaged by a stray bomb from an American plane. The pilot just dropped his last bomb as he came over the town and it happened to land on my school, though luckily it was at a weekend. This meant I had to attend the other senior school in Ceské Budějovice which was Roman Catholic and run by nuns. Contrary to everybody's beliefs, nuns are not very good. They seemed to me to be resentful that they were teaching and caring for children when they couldn't have any of their own. Although the nuns didn't lay a finger on us their punishments were cruel when we did something disagreeable such as fidget or fail to pay attention. We were then placed in the corner of the room and told to kneel on hard, dried peas or wooden slats – it got pretty painful. When I told my mother she wouldn't believe that nuns would act like that but when she heard my stories corroborated by other pupils and their mothers she promptly took me out of that school. I then continued my lessons at home by having work sent to me or collected. I preferred that and I became very quick at completing it so that I had plenty of time to myself.

I can remember visiting Hungary with my mother when I was about seven. We probably travelled using the railway passes my father was allocated from his work. We went to see her younger sister, my Auntie Anna Fischbäckova, who was working in Budapest for a Jewish family who ran a business, possibly a clothing business, though I am not sure. Auntie Anna called herself a governess though I now believe that she was really more

Anna Erika's Confirmation, 1939.

of a nursery nurse or nanny. She cared for four children aged fours years to twelve or thirteen and I believe she did teach them a little and I should think that would have been to practise their German or Czech languages. It wasn't the done thing for us to meet her employers so she made arrangements for us to stay at a house nearby.

To me Budapest seemed a huge city with absolutely massive buildings. It was something out of this world to a seven year old. I remember walking across the main bridge in the city. Buda is one side and Pest is on the other.

Passport photos of parents, Marie and Frantisek Jenne, stamped for visits to Budapest 1935 and 1937.

During her time off work Auntie Anni, as we called her, showed us around and even took us to a swimming baths. I had never before seen one. It was a huge place. Auntie Anni made my mother and I go into the water as well. We knew how to swim because in summertime we swam in the lake in front of our house. We wore swimming costumes whilst everyone else, including my aunt, swam in the nude! We thought that was rather odd.

By the 1930s Budapest had a chic Bohemian culture. It was a city of café and restaurant societies where writers, artists, poets and the avant-garde enjoyed music, gypsy or jazz, and cabaret. Unconventional and outlandish morés were practised, nudity and nude bathing being two of them. Women dared to go without underwear, wore bold coloured clothing with a gypsy look, or had short bobbed hair. Anna Fischbäckova developed some of these traits, which she retained until the day she died.

I can't remember ever having met my Auntie Anni before this time. I was born in 1930 and she had left Rudolfov for her work during the 1920s when she was only eighteen or nineteen. From what is written on the back of her photograph, she was in the north-eastern Hungarian city of Nyiregyhaza in 1928, and perhaps that's where she got her first job, though she was in Budapest by 1930 when she became a Godmother to me by proxy and gave me my second name – Erika. Little did we know that in the distant future she would get her wish for that to become my first name.

Anna Marie Fischbäckova, in Nyiregyhaza, north east Hungary, 1928.

CHAPTER THREE
THE SECOND WORLD WAR BEGINS

I CAN JUST ABOUT remember that my mother once took me to Vienna but we had no difficulty with the language. As far as I can remember our mixed Czech and German community all lived quite happily until the War which started with the German occupation in March 1939. Even then I can't remember any conflict, though as a child I wasn't really interested in what was happening. I just continued to have a happy time at school and at home our parents kept us away from any problems. We heard there were German soldiers in Prague and the bigger towns but we were in a small village, and even the nearest town of Ceské Budëjovice was not that big, so we didn't have German occupation properly until about 1941. We were not bothered by the German soldiers even though they were billeted in the village in the crenellated 'castle' which they used as their Headquarters. I think it was a munitions arsenal too. German soldiers would arrive, stay a while, then they would march off. We even had a German Officer's wife stay in our house for a few months, and her husband stayed with her on the odd occasion. They were kind to us and we could communicate because we spoke the language and we didn't feel any barrier. We had no hardship, so I can't say the German soldiers were bad to us. We were not frightened of them at all but we never saw any SS men come into our village. Our parents did warn us to stay away from soldiers wearing black uniforms and I did spot one once in Ceské Budëjovice. For the whole time, right up to the end of the War in 1945, to me everything just went on normally. All I knew was that our part of Czechoslovakia had become a 'Protectorate' of the Germans called Bohmen und Mahren – Bohemia and Moravia. Our currency was changed and there were extra street signs in German – Rudolfov had the added name of Rudolfstadt and Ceské Budëjovice became Budweis, although some street signs in the dual languages were already present before the War.

I do remember once when Hitler visited Ceské Budëjovice my father was listening to a commentary on the radio which became obscured every now and again by interference. I realise now that the 'interference' was in fact cheering from the crowd who wanted to become totally German, living so close to the border as we did.

The area of north-western Czechoslovakia was known as the Sudetenland. This was part of Germany until 1806 and between 1815 and 1866. After the First World War this 11,000 square mile area, where ninety percent of the inhabitants were ethnic Germans, became part of the newly formed Czechoslovakia. It had a very successful economy from its glass works, textile, pencil, paper-making, toy-making, chemical and coal mining industries until the World Recession of the late 1920s and 1930s caused its local and export trade to collapse and many lost their livelihoods. Consequently, many ethnic Germans looked even more towards Germany where Hitler was developing 'jobs for all' as he ploughed government money into the development of his 'war machine'. This caused continued political agitation and social unrest in this unstable land of the borders, leading to its annexation in 1938 by Nazi Germany, and their eventual total invasion of the whole of Czechoslovakia in 1939.

In 1943 when Walter was almost fifteen he got a scholarship to attend a four year course at the Cartography School in Prague as he was clever at drawing and was a good scholar. I remember visiting him with my mother when he showed us some of his sketches and maps. I believe by that time it was a German-run school or college but Walter was unable to complete more than two years of his Course because the Germans were by then losing the War and they conscripted him into their Army.

Walter Jenne in German Army uniform, 1945.

My father was too old to be conscripted by the Germans but my half-brothers and sisters were obliged to work for them. The youngest, Karl, enlisted or was conscripted into the Ground Staff of the German Luftwaffe, being a blonde boy, the only blonde in the family. He was a lovely looking fellow. He was sent to the Leipzig area where he met a German girl, Hilde, whom he married in 1942. I remember him bringing his new wife home to meet us and my father giving him a good ticking off because she had become pregnant before the marriage. Karl, by that time, was a man of twenty-one! Hilde was eventually welcomed as part of our family. I now notice that in the

photograph taken just after his marriage, Karl is wearing the Iron Cross medal. He must have done something brave to receive it. When or how he achieved this, my remaining family do not know. Living in Soviet controlled East Germany as he did after the War, perhaps he threw it away, fearing the Stasi Communist Police who often searched people's homes.

Frank became a hairdresser for the German Army. Mitzi did secretarial work and Klara was a dressmaker. They were safe, and so were their husbands, but they were actually in a sort of 'forced labour'. Their work

Karl Jenne in Luftwaffe Uniform, Ground Staff, 1942.

was now under total German rule, not as they had previously worked, being near the border, where there had been half Czech and half German employers. They got paid, but not as much as before the War. I assume it was because the Germans wanted us to be aware that we were now under the rule of Germany that they issued bank notes printed with both languages. Korun (Crown) was Czech and Kronen was German. On these notes was written: 'under the protectorate of Böhmen und Mähren' which meant in Czech the 'Protectorate of Bohemia and Moravia'.

Protectorate of Bohemia and Moravia 50 Kronen banknote.

Perhaps it was due to the influence of the German Officer and his wife who stayed at our house from time to time that in 1942 my father was made one of the Bürgermeisters of our village and worked at the small village offices. This job would be similar to a Parish Leader in this country. My father had always been interested in the village life in relation to treating everybody the same, regardless of whether they were Czech or German. He dealt with complaints from the village people and helped to sort out any disputes. He was a pacifier or peace-keeper – that's how I think of my father in those days. By this time he was around fifty-six years old and I think for a while he continued to work part-time as the Freight Stationmaster at Ceské Budějovice. Looking back, I have a feeling he was moved from being Freight Manager because the Germans preferred to have one of their soldiers in charge. Whether he ever saw any evidence of Jewish people being transported in cattle trucks to be 're-settled' I do not know. If he did, he never spoke about it, even to the time of his death.

Of course, it is now known that the Jews were transported to death camps and not to be 're-settled' at all! Had my father suspected any of this activity, rather than play a part, he was the type of person who might have requested a change of job to Bürgermeister.

There was only one Jewish family in Rudolfov. They were owners of a shop near to the church and the school. I think their children had grown up. I can remember he was the kindest man. He must have been in his fifties, and to me he was a nice old man. When we had some money to buy sweeties he always put one or two more into the little home-made paper bag. One day I went to his shop and he was wearing a yellow star and arm band. When I asked my parents what this was they told me it was because he was a Jew. I asked "What is a Jew?" I knew he looked a little bit different but I didn't know why. My parents explained that Jews had a different religion. Then the family were taken away suddenly and the shop was closed. This was probably in 1942. We asked our parents what had happened to them but they protected us and didn't want us to know of any 'bad goings-on'. We just had to find another sweetie shop which was further away and was in a grocer's shop. It was run by a family called Srp and I was in school with the daughter who always let me know when there was a supply of sweeties in her father's shop. The Jew's shop in Rudolfov remained empty.

We did notice that there were a few clothes shops which might have been run by Jews which were closed in Ceské Budějovice and re-opened selling other things. It appeared to me that our area of southern Czechoslovakia was not a place where many Jews settled, so I did not notice that many people were disappearing.

In 1930 there were 80,000 Jews living in Bohemia and Moravia and within Czechoslovakia itself there were 270,000. The majority of these Jews were killed by the Germans by 1945, together with 250,000 Czech Communists, Socialists and Pacifists.

It wasn't until much later in my life that I learnt of the Prisoner of War camps, the German concentration camps and death camps in Poland and other events such as the destruction of the pure Czech villages of Lidice and Lezáky – located so close to me, yet their fate unbeknown to me. This is all so shocking to me.

In retaliation for the assassination in June 1944 of the acting German Protector of Bohemia and Moravia, called 'the Butcher of Prague', Reinhard Heydrich, which was organised by the Czech government-in-exile in London, Hitler ordered the murder of all inhabitants of Lidice and Lezáky – men, women and children. Their villages were then flattened and scorched.

I did get to know that the Germans were very particular about 'clean blood', as they called it, and did not allow any Jewish connections. My father had to produce a family tree, going back to the 1770s, and then complete specially produced Nazi forms to prove that there was no Jewish blood in his nor my mother's families.

It was probably in 1942 that our neighbour, Mr Prochaska, whom I didn't know at the time was my uncle by marriage, was suddenly arrested by German soldiers whilst he was away from home and taken to the concentration camp in Munich called Dachau. I do remember German soldiers coming to search their house. All I was told was that he was an 'underground worker' who had been taking messages backwards and forwards, though to whom, at the time, I hadn't a clue. In retrospect, he was most probably working 'underground' for the Czech Resistance for he was definitely a full-blooded Czech – not like

Last page of family tree dating back to 1770 on special Nazi form.

the rest of my family whom I knew. At the time we children wondered why he was arrested but never found out. I vaguely remember that there were other people from my village who just disappeared and were never heard of again. I imagine they were also Czech Resistance workers.

Mr Prochaska's wife and their children, Antonia and Rudi were very upset when he suddenly disappeared. In early June 1945, he returned, a broken man. I can only surmise that he was liberated by the Americans at the end of the War. I didn't know what torture he had endured in Dachau but he was 'skin and bone' and he would shut himself in his house, not venturing out at all. He just sat by his stove warming himself. The only person he spoke to was his wife.

There was one other relative of ours who disappeared in the middle of the War. He was my Auntie Elfrieda's husband, Mr Smisek. In 1934, at the age of four, I was their bridesmaid. Mr Smisek was a strapping fellow of over six foot and that's what sticks in my memory. He was a 'traveller' or Sales Rep for the Bata shoes company. He was politically such a staunch Czech who worked away from home most of the time, and this caused a bit of a rift in their marriage. One day my Auntie Frieda, as we called her, was informed that he had been arrested for being a political activist. He was eventually sent to a concentration camp where he died. Their son, Karel Leo, later known as Charles, was to become very close to me.

Towards the end of the War my Auntie Frieda had a relationship with a German Officer. It was not until after the War when he helped her move to Eisenach at a time when German Czechs were being forcibly expelled, that she discovered he was actually already married. This upset and affected her so much that she never had another relationship in her life.

Anna Erika in back garden, Rudolfov, early 1945.

Left to right; Toni, Rudi, Auntie Wittek, Auntie Marie, Anna Erika standing, early 1945.

84

CHAPTER FOUR
THE END OF THE SECOND WORLD WAR
– INVASION BY THE RUSSIANS

I REALLY CAN'T REMEMBER my parents being worried about what would happen if Germany lost the War though I was influenced by the fact that they were trying to protect me. I remember certain names being mentioned, such as Hitler, Mussolini, Italy, but subconsciously I believe I wanted to close it all from my mind. At the time I was pre-occupied with the surprise news that my mother was going to have a baby. I remember seeing my mother crying on several occasions but she would not tell me the reason until one day, when we were returning on the train from visiting her relations in the Bohemian Forest, she told me she was going to have a baby. This was during February 1945, just three months before the baby was born. Although there was to be a big gap of fifteen years between myself and the new baby, I was overjoyed, but when my older brother Walter heard about it he was disgusted; perhaps, at the time, a typical response from a seventeen year old son.

The first indication that things were going very wrong for the Germans was the fact that I could feel fear in the air. My parents and the villagers lived in fear and disappointment because they thought that at the end of the War things would return to the way they were.

I remember my father saying that the Russians were coming nearer and that they were 'doing bad things' though I never heard the details. I remember on my fifteenth birthday, the 8th May 1945, walking to the main road and seeing German soldiers, some wounded, being marched through our village with Russians walking either beside them or behind them, just marching them on. They looked in despair because they were prisoners – the Russian soldiers were their masters now.

I now think they were probably being marched towards the German border, or to a camp of some sort, but as far as I can remember there was no camp in my village. The German soldiers who were billeted at the 'castle' in my village were some of the first to go. Once the Germans had all been removed, the Russians moved into that building. They were marauding and they were not nice people – not nice at all. The terror for us only started when the Russians walked in.

My father, being one of the three Bürgermeisters of our village, witnessed the chaotic infiltration of the council offices and all its paperwork, and he said the Russians didn't have a clue what they were looking for and appeared like children playing havoc with nobody in charge. They instigated a curfew and they looted and stole whatever they wanted from our shops and homes. I remember them shouting "Davi, Davi" (dawaj, dawaj) which means "give, give". I shall never forget those words. If we didn't give them whatever they wanted they just took it, as they pushed us aside or slapped us. They took our possessions, watches and anything that sparkled which caught their eyes. They took just about anything and nearly everything – bedding, chickens, rabbits, food supplies, and I remember some meat which they took from our pantry which they ate raw with their hands in front of us. We thought that was most uncivilised.

The Russians pillaged whatever they took a fancy to and that included women and girls – they just raped them – in their homes or elsewhere. They also went through people's houses abducting young girls to 'work' for them to do their cooking, washing and cleaning and to sexually abuse them. They even made them dig trenches for latrines and kept them away from their families. Many of my girlfriends from my school class were taken away and only three of them were ever seen again. Their parents did not know where they had been taken and they were distraught.

When my parents heard about this they hid me in the hayloft in the roof of our house. From the outside, our house looked more like a one-storey building and from the inside the access was not obvious, so I was temporarily safe there. I had a kerosene lamp and some light from openings at either end of the loft and was surrounded by hay bales. I had to come down on the odd occasions but most of the time I just read, did school-work or did a bit of sewing, knitting or crochet to keep myself occupied.

I had been in the hayloft for three weeks when on the evening of the 28th May my mother went into labour. Because my father was a Bürgermeister the Russians were keeping him occupied at all hours. Auntie Wittek was old, frail and had elderly dementia, so I was the only person able to fetch the midwife, Frau Vandas, who lived on the other side of the village. My heart was pounding as I left the house at around 10pm, breaking the curfew, though at least this was under cover of darkness. I took an indirect route across fields to avoid any Russian soldiers and eventually arrived safely at the midwife's home. I remember shivering and being very frightened and could hardly get my words out but, of course, as soon as she saw me she knew she was needed. My mother at the time was forty, and in those days that was quite an age to have a baby. Frau Vandas and I made the same return journey, evading the Russians. My baby sister, Helene Anna, was born on my parents' bed in the kitchen at about two minutes before midnight. My job was to boil water and fetch towels. I had managed to fetch the midwife just in time and I was absolutely delighted to have a baby sister. My father was not released from his work for the Russians and did not return until two or three days after she was born.

When my little sister was about two weeks old two Russians soldiers entered our house at a time when my mother was breast-feeding. I had come down from the hayloft for some reason or other, probably because I was getting hungry. My mother and I were both accosted. At that moment my father arrived home and instantly pleaded with them to go, or to take him away instead of assaulting my mother or me. He tried to explain in a language foreign to them that my mother had recently had a baby and I was just a young girl – though, of course, they could see this. He offered them anything they wanted from our house if they would leave us alone. I thought I was going to be beaten and my situation became desperate. My mother was saved, though I was not, and eventually they did leave. It was very brave of my father to take a stand against the Russians who were carrying guns. That was the most terrifying day for us all. I still cry when I think of my own extreme fear, the way my mother consoled and attended to me, and my parents' heartbreak.

My father tried to protect all his family, as well as the families in the village. As a Bürgermeister he felt he had a duty but unfortunately, most of the time, the Russians took no notice of that. There was no-one to complain to because there was no-one in command or with authority. He felt he should go to a Judge or Priest but perhaps by then they had no authority either. My father was a broken man, having to watch all this happening, as many husbands, fathers and brothers did. Most of the time they were powerless. I believe that most of the females in my family were raped by Russian soldiers. Years after the War, even until they died, not one of them ever spoke about the 'bad times'. They only ever spoke about the happier times before the War.

My parents began to feel very worried about my future safety. My mother, who pledged no repetition of my torture, heard that there were no Russian soldiers at an isolated farm about ten miles away from our village. By chance, my mother knew the farmer's wife from years before when they had worked together at the Westen Enamel Factory in Ceské Budějovice. My mother decided she would take me there. This was in mid June of 1945 and the curfew was still in existence. She and I started our journey at around four o'clock in the morning, leaving my baby sister, Helli, at home in the care of my father. We walked across fields, up hills, down small country lanes, through woods, over streams and eventually arrived at the farmhouse in a small hamlet called Cerveny Ujest, which means 'little red place'. My mother just knocked on the door and promptly asked for her daughter to be cared for and, of course, the family agreed. Having deposited me, my mother then walked all the way home alone. She took her life in her own hands to save me. She was worrying she might be spotted and arrested by the Russians and in the knowledge that my baby sister would soon be needing a breast-feed.

The couple at the farm spoke Czech but also a little German, and were very kind to me, the wife particularly so. They had three children older than myself, a boy and two girls, but they took me in as one of their own. I helped on the farm or in the house doing whatever I was asked because I was pleased to be safe. I never saw a Russian soldier in the whole of the time I was there but I never left this farmhouse nor its yard with the big wooden gates which were always kept closed. There was another farm about a half an hour's walk away but we never came into contact with the owners. If the farmers themselves met up in the fields, they never said. Nothing was ever talked about at the breakfast or dinner table in relation to what or who was seen. Their parents, like my parents, just protected their children from 'bad news'.

Life on this farm was like going back in time. There was no electricity, and any machinery they had was hand-driven. One of my jobs was to get water for the house or the animals from a pump-well. I was taught to milk the cows and clean them out, then empty the

The farmhouse at Cerveny Ujezdec, previously called Cerveny Ujest.

wheelbarrow full of manure onto a great heap in the centre of the yard. I helped to make sauerkraut, or separate corn from the husk, I minced up swedes and potatoes and fed this to the animals, or assisted with the washing of clothes using a scrubbing board and a large bar of soap. I then immersed the washing into a large wooden tub full of hot water.

In the evenings I sat de-husking goose feathers to make pillows and duvets, some of which were to be sold, so the best feathers and down went into those. There was no radio nor newspapers, so we were totally cut off. I felt as though I was in a different country, in a different century, but nevertheless, I felt safe and I remained at the farmhouse for almost six months.

My mother visited me on a few occasions, once to tell me of the death of Auntie Wittek, which saddened me. In early December she came to tell me that her younger sister, my Auntie Anni, had got in touch with her through the International Red Cross Tracing and Communication Service and that she was coming to visit and, if possible, take me back to England with her. I was astounded and couldn't speak for quite a while, worrying why I should have to go so far away after I had been saved in hiding. I hadn't met Auntie Anni since I was seven when I went to Budapest with my mother and I had no idea she was now living in England. I was now fifteen-and-a-half and was not very happy about leaving my family and my country. My mother told me she would return to the farm to fetch me as soon as my Auntie Anni arrived from England, so I at least had time to say my goodbyes to the kind people on the farm who had taken me in and of whom I had become quite fond.

Just before Christmas 1945 my mother arrived and we walked home to Rudolfov at around midnight but at the time, from what I remember, there was no curfew. It was just safer to walk in the dark, but the situation was a little more settled then. There was more organisation and discipline, not only from the Russian Army but also from the Czech people who were trying to run their own government. As we walked in the freezing snow my mother tried to reassure me that my stay in England would be for a short time until things had settled to the way they were before the War.

Anna Erika with cousin Toni, Christmas 1945, Rudolfov.

CHAPTER FIVE
BENEVOLENCE FROM BOURNEMOUTH

ANNA MARIE FISCHBÄCKOVA, PRONOUNCED Fischböckova, was born in the little village of Mugrau in the Bohemian Forest in 1909. Her father, Franz was Austro-Hungarian and her mother, Paulina, born Gutschkova, was German. Anna had an older brother and sister, Joseph and Marie and younger siblings, Henry and Elfrieda. The family moved to Rudolfov, Czechoslovakia, after the First World War. By 1928, at the age of nineteen, Anna was working as a nursery assistant in Hungary in the north-eastern city of Nyiregyhaza, although by 1930 she was a nanny-au pair for a Jewish Hungarian family who ran a business in Budapest. The type of business is not known.

Anna Marie Fischbäckova, Budapest, 1938.

From 1933 when Hitler came to power anti-semitism became a major concern. In 1938 the darkest days for the Jews were dawning causing Anna's Jewish employers in Budapest to make a life-changing decision to emigrate to safety in the USA. Their nursery nurse, Anna Fischbäckova, was asked to go with them. We do not know the route they took but in the spring or summer of 1939 they eventually reached the shores of England where they stayed on the south coast waiting for an 'allocation' of a ship to America from Southampton. At this time the major Allied countries had stringent immigration quota systems. The only year in which immigration of the entire quotas for the United States was reached, was in 1939. Thereafter, only around twenty-five percent of applications were accepted. Non-Jewish emigrants of German descent faced a major hurdle in proving themselves anti-Nazi. Those seeking re-emigration were often interned until their 'quota' permit became available, although those with relatives or friends already in this country might take advantage of their hospitality and sponsorship and thus avoid this fate. On 1 September 1939 the Germans invaded Poland which brought the British and other Allies into the War, although not the Americans until the aerial invasion of their fleet by the Japanese at Pearl Harbour in Hawaii on 7 December 1941. Once Britain had declared war with Germany the ongoing passage for re-emigrants to USA or Israel was delayed, sometimes for the duration of the War. Anna's Jewish ex-employers did arrive in USA although it is not known in which year. Whatever the situation, Anna was left behind and became a non-Jewish German Refugee in this country. As such, she would have been assisted by one of the many charitable Refugee Committees and could have been offered hostel accommodation in Bournemouth.

Anna Marie Fischbäckova with Jewish children in her care, Isle of Wight, Summer 1939.

Anna could speak German, Czech, Hungarian and a little English. At a Refugee Tribunal her credentials and political preference would have been examined. She was given permission to remain in England as a 'Friendly Alien' and required to present herself regularly at a Bournemouth police station to confirm details of her address and employment. The Bournemouth Quakers Society of Friends set up an educational centre in Avenue Road, close to the centre of Bournemouth, where they taught English to Refugees. Nearby, in Surrey Road, the Bournemouth Central Committee for Refugees maintained a hostel to provide 'training' and accommodation for the 'Friendly Aliens'. Anna became proficient in English although she was never to lose her German-Czech accent. There was "a procession of Germans visiting the Quakers in Avenue Road" – as reported in the local press. In addition, in Suffolk Road there was a branch of the YWCA offering assistance and accommodation.

After the British declared war with Germany on 6 September 1939, 'Friendly Aliens' were placed into categories – those who had lived in England for at least six years, and a category for those who had lived here for less time. Those in the latter category had their movements restricted by a curfew and were unable to own a car, bicycle or a radio. There was also a 'high risk' category. However, by May 1940 there was a drastic reversal of British policy due to the panic caused by the German advances across western Europe which the Allies felt had been assisted by 'Fifth Columnists' and German spies. Consequently, an Order was issued for the internment of all categories. This, of course, included Anna. We do not know when she was arrested or released. My research at the National Archives revealed nothing. Either the records were destroyed, or they have not yet been released. However, the strict regulations began to be relaxed in the late autumn and by 1941 most internees who were considered not to be a risk to security were released.

An act of good fortune led to Anna Fischbäckova meeting the elderly bachelor, Mr Arthur Vincent Aston-Nicholas. Had she been resident at the YWCA hostel in Suffolk Road and employed in domestic work at the boarding house at number eight? We do not know. Domestic work was the only occupation permitted to female 'Friendly Aliens' before and post-internment. The method of securing Anna's release from internment is not known. One might assume that Mr Aston-Nicholas had friends in high places. Applications for internees to marry took months to be processed. Nevertheless, on 5 September 1940 Arthur Vincent Aston-Nicholas married Anna, by now known as 'Annie' Fischbäck, at Bournemouth Registry Office. She was thirty-one and he gave his age as sixty-eight, although he was in fact eighty-two. On their marriage certificate they both gave their address as number eight, Suffolk Road, which was the boarding house. Throughout her whole life Anna never told her family nor her friends how they met, nor did she speak of him, although she did tell them she had been interned. The family believe she had not wished to reveal her husband's true age, and they also consider she knew little about his background. At the making of his Will, nine days before his death in 1942, he stated he was a retired art teacher of the Glasgow School of Art. According to the family, had Anna known of the prominence of the Glasgow School of Art, she might have been tempted to boast to them later in her life.

After the marriage the couple moved close-by to the top two floors of a large detached Edwardian house called 'White Gables' at 29 Queen's Road, Westbourne, which they furnished in a desirable fashion. The previous occupant of this large apartment had been the ageing widow, Viscountess the Right Honourable Mabel Augustus Frankfort de Montmorency. It was here that Annie set up a business providing bed and breakfast for long-term British 'well-do-do' paying guests. She anglicised her first name to Ann and also resurrected her sewing skills to become a peripatetic dressmaker and seamstress to a high-class clientele.

Bournemouth experienced many German bombing raids as the War raged on but there was an air raid shelter close-by at 21 Queen's Road. On 17 April 1942 Arthur Vincent Aston-Nicholas died from chronic bronchitis, emphysema and influenza, aged eighty-four. In his Will he left his young widow with what was at the time a considerable inheritance of one thousand, two hundred and sixteen pounds, ten shillings and two pence. Arthur was buried in consecrated land at Wimborne Road Cemetery although there was no head-stone. The cost of the burial ground was four pounds and four shillings but as the land was never purchased there was a rule that no head-stone could be erected, and the Local Authority also had the right, thirty-five years hence, to allow a stranger burial in the same grave, and this did happen in 1977.

The life's work of Arthur Vincent Aston-Nicholas had been famously executed and his contribution to the development of the Arts and Crafts, and to the Industry of this country, brilliantly achieved. We can only assume that his betrothal had been a 'marriage of benevolence' or convenience, for Annie probably cared for Arthur during their eighteen-month marriage, and she was with him when he died. Nevertheless, he had not only rescued her from internment, he had given her the security of a British passport, an inheritance, a pension, and the opportunity to follow two careers. For Anna, the last three years of the War, and her life henceforth, was comfortable.

When the War in Europe drew to an end in May 1945, and the War in the Far East by August, Mrs Anna Aston-Nicholas sought news of her family in war-torn Czechoslovakia through the International Red Cross Tracing and Communication Service based in Geneva. By 8 August 1945 she was able to exchange letters with her beloved siblings and learnt of their terrible plight due to the aggressive invasion by the Russians. Consequently, she decided to personally do something about it. Anna Aston-Nicholas was on a mission to assist her family. One of her nieces, Anna Erika Jennova, was then fifteen.

Just before Christmas 1945 Auntie Anni arrived in Rudolfov having flown into Prague and taken the train or bus to Ceské Budëjovice. I don't think she was ever frightened of anything or anyone. She was an over-powering type of person. When she strode in, everybody stopped. As far as we were concerned she had a British passport and she was rich! She was handing out cigarettes by the dozen — that was how she paid for a lot of things, even with the Russian soldiers. I remember her putting her arms around me and saying "You're going to be safe now". The memory of her saying that makes me cry, even now.

Left to right; Toni, Pepi, Anna Erika, Auntie Anni and Rudi. The night before Anna Erika left for England, January 1946.

I remember spending Christmas 1945, my last in Czechoslovakia, at home with my family in Rudolfov and that was wonderful. It was a joy to see my little sister, Helli, who was by then six months' old. Sadly, my brother, Walter, whom I hadn't seen for almost a year, wasn't there. As an ex-German Army soldier he had been forced by the Russians to work as a labourer wherever he was needed, though we didn't know that then. I met up with our next-door neighbours, Toni and Rudi, whom I discovered years later were actually my cousins. I saw my mother's sister, Auntie Frieda and her brothers, Uncle Henry and Uncle Joe. I more or less had time to say goodbye to all of them, even to my half-brother and sisters, Klara, Mitzi and Frank. Karl was not there. He had enlisted or been conscripted into the German Air Force and was in a small place called Zerbst Anhalt near Leipzig. After the War's end he quickly changed to wearing 'civvies' so as not to be classified as a soldier. He and Hilde had two sons, Gerhard and Karl Heinz, and they lived for the rest of their lives in this town in the Russian controlled zone of Germany.

All the family came to see me because it was definitely a big secret in the village that I was at home, so I daren't go out. I wanted to stay in the house and not have to hide in the loft again. Russian soldiers were still around though the uncouth ones seemed to have moved on into mainland Germany. Auntie Anni brought some foods from England that I had not seen for a long time, including bananas and oranges. I didn't know how she managed to buy them in England because just post-war I believe they still weren't generally available there – but she did – and she brought them to Czechoslovakia! She had also managed to procure, from Prague or from Ceské Budĕjovice, official 'papers' for me so that she could take me from the country and enter England with me in tow. Perhaps she even stated that I was an orphan, I just do not know.

We had our traditional fast throughout the day on Christmas Eve, followed in the evening by our meal of carp-fish fried in breadcrumbs and accompanied by green and potato salads. The fish from the village lake had been kept alive from before the winter freeze in a wooden tub in the wash-house. Christmas Eve was the most important day of Christmas.

Of course, I thought that saying my 'goodbye' meant I would be seeing the family members again in a short time because I was told by my parents that I would be returning as soon as things became more settled. I was not to guess that they would in fact get worse.

On the morning of the 14th January 1946 Auntie Anni and I trundled with our suitcases and things on a little handcart into Ceské Budějovice railway station. My mother carried baby Helli because the snow was too deep to push a pram. My mother gave us sandwiches and cold tea which is what we used to drink in those days. My father had made sure we had seats on the train. They waved goodbye to us from the platform. Even today, I cry every time I think of that.

The journey to Prague took a couple of hours and we arrived at the main station which was opposite St. Wenceslas Square. We stayed at the Station Hotel, just across the road to the right. We were to have flown out on the 16th January but the weather was very bad and flights were cancelled for six days so we had to stay at the hotel longer than anticipated, but my aunt had enough money to support that. Strangely, there was hardly anybody around in Prague. We just walked around and had our meals in cafés. There was food available if you had coupons and my aunt had procured plenty of those, though I don't know how – perhaps on the 'black market'. Parts of Prague were very badly damaged – not just due to the Allied bombing but to the internal fighting between the Germans and Russians at the end of the War. In the old town, if I remember correctly, there was a crater in the middle of the square near to the church with the two towers and the clock with the moving figures, which wasn't working. It was working when I was there with my mother in 1944 to visit my brother Walter at his cartography school. Auntie Anni and I walked around Prague to pass the time

and to see as much as we could. Only 'the powers that be' of Auntie Anni could do that!

Eventually we travelled to the airport by bus and we boarded a Dakota aeroplane at around lunchtime. It was a transport plane with seats either side, not rows of seats across, and it was very basic with no lining whatsoever. From the air the bombed sites looked gruesome over Germany and across Belgium. London seemed particularly bad. Again I was lucky when Auntie Anni requested for me to go and stand next to the pilot. When we crossed the English Channel it was the first time in my life I had seen the sea. It was definitely an adventure for me. The pilot was British, but without a uniform, and he was wearing a peaked cap of some sort. There was no stewardess or steward. There were only about four other adult passengers on the flight and there were another six or eight seats empty. I remember one man had a briefcase. My aunt talked to them all. A Dakota is not that big, and I don't believe there was a toilet on the plane, or one was not pointed out to me. I didn't notice if there was any cargo. All I was concerned about was that I was on a plane and I was going to England.

Research informs me that only the 'rich and connected' could organise a flight from England to Prague in the December of 1945. Commercial flights from Croydon to Prague did not resume after the end of the War until 1 August 1946 when the price for a sixty-day return ticket was thirty-two pounds and eight shillings and a single fare was eighteen pounds. However, Anna Aston-Nicholas managed to procure a return seat on a DC3 Dakota transport-plane which flew to Prague a few days before Christmas 1945. This was against all odds since millions of troops, ex-prisoners of war, refugees and displaced persons were on the move throughout Europe, either by transport-plane, train, boat, truck, or on foot.

In no time we seemed to land at Croydon airport. We travelled by taxi to Swiss Cottage in London to stay with my aunt's friend who, by her accent, sounded as though she came from Austria. I think she was a widow who had no children. She made me very welcome and plied me with all sorts of things that I had never seen in my life before. I had a bedroom of my own and was tucked in with blankets which I couldn't bear because I had only ever been used to duvets.

After a few days we took the train to Westbourne, a railway station which has now been demolished. I was overwhelmed by travelling on the underground across London to Waterloo. Also by the wide avenues of Bournemouth. From West Station we then walked for only about two minutes to 'White Gables', 29 Queen's Road. I was amazed just how big the house was. My aunt lived in the top two floors of this three-storey detached Edwardian house. The entrance to the ground floor apartment was at the back of the house in Suffolk Road, as the house was situated on a corner. It felt massive and beautiful and beautifully furnished, with lovely carpets on the floor. On the first floor, up the main staircase, there were four bedrooms, a big lounge-dining room, a bathroom and two toilets. There was also an outside emergency staircase leading up to the kitchen which had a gas stove. On the top floor there were two bedrooms, another toilet and a bathroom combined. I had never seen a bathroom before, nor an inside toilet except at the home of my aunt's friend in Swiss Cottage. I was staggered to see there were two bathrooms and two toilets. Using a proper bath for the very first time felt like I was at the swimming baths only with running hot water and electricity. My aunt had acquired some clothing and shoes of red leather for me.

Of course it felt very strange to be in a land where all the streets had pavements, and I couldn't speak the language, but my aunt told me that if I didn't learn to speak English quickly then I would be lost, though I did in fact find it quite easy. My aunt gave me lessons at every opportunity, speaking as well as written. She made me copy articles from newspapers or read aloud to her and I began to memorise the spellings. Every evening I was made to sit down and practise writing English in the same way that my father had made me practise my German and Czech writing back home. My English pronunciations had to be correct, for she was a good teacher. I still thank her for the English I speak now though strangely she herself had a Czech-German accent all her life. After about six months she enrolled me at Bournemouth College, Lansdowne to study English and Art at evening classes and in eighteen months I learnt a lot. I especially loved Art and became quite good at it, but Auntie Anni thought I couldn't earn a living from it, so I had to give it up.

For two-and-a-half years, to earn my keep I waited on my aunt's lodgers at breakfast-time, made the beds and generally cleaned. Having had to do so much housework whilst in hiding at the Czech farm, I was quite happy to do it again – only in better surroundings. I also learnt to cook the English way. My aunt looked after her paying guests well enough, though we had to be a little bit frugal for ourselves because Auntie Anni knew how to look after her pennies. I was also sent on errands to the shops and would have to memorise the correct English words for my purchases. I was not allowed to make a written list. In many ways my aunt was quite strict, and everything had to be done 'her way', especially when it came to needlework. I had already done a little sewing at the knee of the dressmaker who used to come to our house in Rudolfov so I was soon able to come up to the high standards of Auntie Anni.

The task I really enjoyed was taking my aunt's dog, Sally, for walks. I loved ambling down Queen's Road, to Overcliff Drive or Alum Chine, just ten minutes to the sea-front. I was always absolutely enthralled by the sound of the waves on the sand. I felt privileged, I felt safe, but I was lonely, thinking of those I had left behind. Up until the time I was married I had to visit the local Police Station every month, then every six months, to sign as an 'Alien'.

As a dressmaker my aunt had acquired a 'well-to-do' clientele and friends who knew her as Ann. Since I had the same name, when they came for afternoon tea, or we visited for a fitting, they started to call her 'old Ann' and me 'young Ann' which she did not like. So she felt this had to change. I was Christened Anna Erika Henrietta Renate, Erika being chosen by my aunt — so 'Erika' I was to be from then on. Luckily it was the name I preferred and have been known by ever since. Auntie Anni became Auntie Annie at home.

Erika (Anna now dropped) in England, 1946.

At the end of the War President Edvard Benes returned to Czechoslovakia from his government-in-exile in London. The Potsdam Conference in 1945 determined that Sudeten Germans would have to leave Czechoslovakia. Following the Benes decrees in 1946 the majority were expelled. These expulsions included most of the Jenne and the Fischbäck families. Only proven anti-fascists and forced labourers were allowed to stay. Over three million ethnic Germans were evicted to the American, French or British-controlled zones of West Germany, to Austria or to Soviet controlled East Germany. Their properties were confiscated and taken over by pure Czechs, Slovaks, Gypsies and, for a while, Hungarians. However, President Benes was unable to stop the tide of Communist influence and the country eventually became a Soviet puppet state. The whole of Eastern Europe, which included Czechoslovakia, was governed or controlled by Communist Russia up until its downfall in 1989.

CHAPTER SIX
REUNION IN BAVARIA, CHRISTMAS 1947

FROM BOURNEMOUTH I WAS able to write to my parents in Rudolfov though firstly my letters were 'inspected' by Auntie Annie and secondly, they were censored by the Communists. I suppose they didn't want people to know how good things were here. When I hear the word 'Communism' I still get a shiver down my back. In her letters to me my mother mentioned that 'we may not stay here much longer'.

A Communist lady officer took a liking to our house at 74 Rudolfov. My parents were given the option of moving into a type of working camp or of leaving the country altogether. They chose the latter, though because my father, being the Bürgermeister, was being held by the Communists at the time, my mother had to leave with little Helli and some neighbours and their children. My mother and little Helli were expelled from our home carrying very few possessions on the 17th May 1946. The train took them to what was called a 'displaced persons' holding camp' at Bad Kissingen in the American Zone of Bavaria. My father, who must have been prevented from leaving with them, was given permission to enter the American Zone on the 4th November 1946. They had lost their home, their furniture, their money and possessions – everything except for a dozen or so small items and some clothing. As very little cash or documents were permitted to be taken from the country, my father put what money he had, together with the Deeds of our house, into a little tin box and buried it behind the wash-house in our garden. A year later, somehow or other, my brother Walter travelled back into Rudolfov, and one night he climbed the back fence with the intention of digging it up. A type of extension had been built, so try as he might, he never found it.

Conditions in the crowded Displaced Persons Unit were not ideal. My mother requested they live in a village somewhere. After a month or so the Americans were able to allocate a small farm in a place near Schweinfurt called Seubrigshausen. Here they lived in a loft space which had one bedroom and one other room. Soon after, Auntie Frieda and her son Karel joined them, so conditions were pretty cramped and terrible. Of course, the language was not a problem for them because they spoke both German and Czech. My father, then aged sixty-one, had to return to his old trade of being a carpenter but he also worked in the fields. Helli was only one year and my mother had to help in the fields or collect wood or mushrooms from the forest. They were desperately poor.

Inlaid marquetry box made in Seubrigshausen by Erika's father.

The whole family, except for Mr Prochaska, his wife Marie and their children, Rudi and Toni, moved out from Czechoslovakia to Bavaria. Mitzi and her husband settled in Ingoldstadt, Klara and her husband in Schweinfurt, and Frank and his wife in Hof. Karl and his wife, Hilde, were near Leipzig in Saxony. My dear brother, Walter, got a job in the coalmines in Essen, further west, where his lovely hands with which he once drew maps became hardened and rough. I shall never forget that. He at least earned enough to send a little money to our parents. My mother's brothers, Frank, Jo and Henry and their families also left behind all their possessions. They were content just to move into Bavaria, close to the boarder with Czechoslovakia, because they hoped that sooner or later they would go back home again.

Mother, Father and sister Helli, Seubrigshausen, 1948/9.

Knowing that my family were now safe I was determined to go to visit them for the Christmas of 1947 for it was now two years since I had last seen them. Although I didn't get paid working for Auntie Annie, probably because she was sending little bits of money to my parents, I had saved a few pennies from doing extra jobs for her lodgers, and Auntie Annie bought my return train ticket to Prague. I was only seventeen-and-a-half but somehow I felt confident travelling alone. I caught the train to Waterloo and then travelled to Victoria Station to get the boat train to Ostend. I was saddened to see the War devastation of Cologne, Frankfurt, and throughout my journey. Passengers travelling all the way to Prague, or returning, did not have permission to leave the train in Germany. At that time nobody was allowed to leave a train in the International Zones when it was travelling to Prague, so I had to travel in the back carriage which did not reach the platform when the train stopped at various stations.

I eventually arrived in Prague, where I got my necessary papers stamped, but I stayed on the station all night waiting for the next train back. Auntie Annie had told me that when that train reached Frankfurt I was to bribe a guard with cigarettes so that he would release my suitcase to me. Suitcases had to be stored in the guard's van and were not allowed in seating areas. I bribed him with ten cigarettes, plus another ten to open the locked door of my carriage which wasn't standing near the platform. I don't know how I managed to climb down to the tracks holding my suitcase and walk across several train lines to get to a platform, but there, waiting for me, was my dear brother, Walter. I was elated. It all seemed so easy. I had anticipated feeling the sort of fear I felt when the Russians invaded, but strangely I didn't. Walter had bought a couple of platform tickets so that we could exit the station. We then walked across fields for about eight kilometres to another station so that we could catch a local train. In Germany they are called bummelbahns. On arrival at a small station it was now late in the evening so we stayed on the platform until dawn and then caught a bus to Seubrigshausen where our mother was waiting for us. I was shocked to see that my mother seemed to have aged so much. She was forty-two but looked seventy. For the previous two years she had had such a hard life.

On arrival at their accommodation on the farm I was appalled by the conditions. It was such a pokey, dirty little place that I called it 'Sauhausen' which in German means

Erika, Father, Mother, Walter, Helli at Seubrigshausen on her visit in 1950.

something like a pig sty. It was wonderful to see my little sister, Helli, who was now two and a half, and my dear father, though he too looked bedraggled and old. It was overwhelming to see them all again and my two week stay, which had been shortened because of my long and convoluted journey, quickly slipped by.

My return journey was less fraught because, having had my papers stamped, I did not need to go back to Prague. My brother Walter purchased platform tickets at Frankfurt and put me on the train coming through from Prague to Cologne. I was told to make sure I sat in a carriage where there were American soldiers, which I did. They were friendly and I told them a little about my plight. When I told them about the discrepancy of the station name on my papers they soon 'adopted' me and told the guard I was travelling with them. So as far as any passport or border checks were concerned I was deemed to be American and my papers weren't requested. I was ill on the boat trip across the Channel due to rough seas and when I finally arrived

Erika and brother, Walter, on her visit to see him in Essen, 1951.

98

back in Bournemouth I found it hard to comprehend what I had achieved by myself. I was told that as a pretty young woman travelling alone I was lucky to have met so many decent people. This gave me the added strength and confidence to overcome any long-term psychological affects caused by the Russian invasion. Perhaps I had inherited my mother's strength and perseverance, for I knew I had to forget in order to go forward with my life.

Erika with Helli and parents, on her visit in 1956.

Walter with girlfriend, near Essen in the 1950s.

CHAPTER SEVEN
THE BOURNEMOUTH PIED PIPER

I WASN'T ABLE TO get a British Work Permit until I was eighteen in May 1948 so until then I remained caring for the lodgers at 29 Queen's Road. Before that though, in 1947, my Auntie Annie decided to rescue my two cousins, Renate, aged thirteen and eleven year-old Elfrieda, or Friedl as we called her. They were the children of her brother, Henry Fischbäck, and his wife Kate. At the time the family had been forced out of Czechoslovakia and were in a 'holding camp' for Displaced Persons in Bavaria awaiting resettlement accommodation, so they obviously gave my aunt permission to bring their children here to a better life until Germany recovered from the War.

I can remember being left in charge of the lodgers in the house, though actually, I suppose, they were in charge of me, but with me doing all the work and looking after them! My aunt travelled to Bavaria by train and was away for around a week or so, also visiting my parents. I was overjoyed to see my two cousins when they arrived. Obviously, they had to learn to speak English immediately and Auntie Annie demanded we only speak English in the home. By her method of teaching they learnt very quickly. After a little while she arranged for them both to attend Bournemouth School for Girls at Lansdowne and until Renate and Friedl were a little older it was my job to walk to and fro with them to this school, some distance away.

Soon after that, one of the gentlemen lodgers died which created a spare room in the house, so Auntie Annie again travelled to Germany, this time to collect her widowed sister, Elfrieda and her thirteen year old son, Karel Leo Smizek, who were both then still squatting with my parents in their cramped allocated accommodation on the farm in Seubrigshausen. At Queen's Road Auntie Frieda slept in a single bed and my cousin, Karel, slept on the floor, though not for long because Auntie Annie soon got Auntie Frieda a job as a cleaning lady for a local dentist where she 'lived in' and Charles, renamed from Karel by my Auntie Annie, was then able to have a room of his own at White Gables. Charles was enrolled at Bournemouth School for Boys at Charminster where he stayed for about eighteen months or so. After about two years Auntie Frieda could speak English well and she got a job as an Auxiliary Nurse in the children's section of Westbourne Hospital where she stayed until she retired.

Charles, Auntie Frieda, Mimi, and Ignatz in Bournemouth, early 1950s.

A little later in 1947 my aunt's brother Joseph Fischbäck, also suffering as a Displaced Person, became very ill living in appalling circumstances in a hut in the woods on a farm near Munich. His wife, Rosie was pregnant at the time so my Auntie Annie travelled to Bavaria, again by train, to collect their two older children, Ignatz and Marie, or Mimi as we called her. I was left in charge of Renate, Friedl, Charles and the boarding house, though by then Charles was quite the 'man of the house' and could do many jobs. We got on very well. Charles' mother, Auntie Frieda visited us when she could afford the bus fares.

It was lovely to have two more young people around the house. Ignatz, renamed by Auntie Annie as Jo, attended a different school to Charles because his school refused to take any more 'foreign boys', as they called them, because of the language difficulties, so he went to St Michael's School in Westbourne. Mimi attended Lansdowne School for Girls. My Auntie Annie arranged all this. She was a great organiser. She even organised the receipt of a weekly 'allowance' for each of us from the Government. She never wanted any children of her own but preferred looking after other people's. However, she was strict and, quite often, more than a little impatient.

By 1949 Uncle Henry and his wife Auntie Kate were really missing their children, Renate and Friedl. Auntie Kate was determined to come to fetch them because they had by then been able to provide a suitable home to be altogether in Linz. However, they did not wish Auntie Annie to incur the further expenses of returning with them. Auntie Kate needed to become employed in order to save this money, and jobs were scarce in Germany. At the time it was impossible for a female married adult from Germany to gain a Work Permit in Britain. Uncle Henry and Auntie Kate therefore decided to divorce, though on what grounds I do not know! As a divorced woman Auntie Kate was able to enter this country and obtain a Work Permit. She stayed with us at Queen's Road for a few days. There was plenty of employment available in hospitals, domestic work or in children's homes at the time and Auntie Annie organised a job for her immediately. She didn't need to know the language to work as a cleaner at Boscombe Hospital and the job was 'living in'. Auntie Annie was amazing. Whatever anybody else tried to do and couldn't, or failed to do — Auntie Annie did!

Auntie Kate worked hard and saved all her earnings and she only saw her children about twice a week because she couldn't afford the bus fares to Queen's Road, but at least she did see them. After six months she had saved enough to take Renate and Friedl to Linz to be reunited with their father, Uncle Henry, whom Auntie Kate quickly remarried. Sadly for them, when Renate and Friedl were a little older they both emigrated from Linz to Toronto, Canada. Renate married a Mr Asghar and had two children, and Friedl married a Mr Cooper and had three children. Toronto is where they all remained.

Renate and Friedl visiting from Canada, c.2003 on their last visit to Linz to sell their deceased parents' house.

When Jo left school in 1950 he got a job as an apprentice undertaking road repairs and learning the building trade. He was getting homesick for his parents and decided to save all his spare money to fund his journey to Bavaria. His father, Uncle Jo, had an operation for cancer of the throat so in August

1952 he felt the time was right to help the family and to meet his younger sister, Anna. They are still very close now. Obviously, he didn't have that much money, and he was reluctant to ask Auntie Annie to buy him a train ticket, so he decided to ride his bike! He cycled totally alone, first to Dover, took a boat to Ostend then followed the quickest route into southern Germany along the Rhine to the woods just outside Munich, which was about eight hundred miles in all. It probably took him about eight days or so, which is good-going, but he was very fit. Once there he helped his father to build a large cabin to replace their shack. This is an amazing story of fortitude and determination in someone the age of seventeen. His sister Mimi decided to remain in Bournemouth because she would have been unable to travel from the woods of Munich to get work. Mimi was rather withdrawn and introspective but she managed to get a job in Bournemouth working for a disabled lady where she helped in the house and took her children to school. She stayed in this country for many years, only moving to Bavaria in around 1963 to be with her parents. She married late in life to a prisoner to whom she had become a pen-friend. The marriage was not a success, but luckily her husband died soon after. Jo, now reverting to being called Ignatz, married Hanelore at the age of twenty-three and had five children. Their second son emigrated to New Zealand, though the others live close by.

Charles and his mother, Auntie Frieda remained in this country all their lives and took British citizenship. Charles got a job with the Bournemouth Electric Company, married an English girl, Mary Able, and they had two daughters, Victoria and Rebecca. Auntie Frieda died in 1986 aged just seventy-one. Sadly, my cousin Charles died in 1996 at the young age of sixty-two.

Of the nine who came, five returned. Auntie Annie, Auntie Frieda, Charles and myself became British citizens because we love this country. Auntie Annie, the 'Pied Piper of Rudolfov' certainly changed our lives, though without the help and inheritance from Mr Arthur Vincent Aston-Nicholas this would not have been possible. Little did he know what his humble benevolence would lead to. And we all knew nothing about him!

CHAPTER EIGHT
THE LIFE IN ENGLAND OF
ERIKA ANNA BROOKE, NÉE JENNOVA

AT THE AGE OF eighteen in May 1948 I was able to get a British Work Permit which was issued at the Foreign Office at High Holborn, London. I had to queue up for two days to get it but luckily Auntie Annie had a friend who lived on Baker Street who put me up for a night. There were plenty of jobs advertised at the office of the Labour Exchange but they were the type of jobs that not everybody wanted to take, such as cleaning or hospital work, jobs that had long hours of up to forty-eight per week or more. My first job, which was living-in, was as a cook-housekeeper to an elderly couple who lived in Ravine Road. I was responsible for all the food and for cleaning the entire house, which was quite an undertaking for an eighteen year-old. Food was still on ration and I learned to be even more frugal myself because I was sending a pound a week to my parents in Germany. However, all my food was included in my wages so I could just afford to do that. As for clothing, even though Auntie Annie was very annoyed with me because I had moved out from White Gables, thus depriving her of rent I could now pay her, she still gave me the odd garment from items sent to her from her pre-War employers who had emigrated to America. I don't know if the Jewish family manufactured the clothing, and I never knew their name or where they lived in America. Garments not used here were sent on by Auntie Annie to our relatives in Germany.

By this time my cousin Charles had moved into a flat in Charminster Road with his mother, my Auntie Frieda, so they too had now become independent. Auntie Kate was here working to save enough money to pay for train tickets to take her children, Renata and Friedl back to Bavaria. Mimi was still at school here, and Ignatz (Jo) was in his last school year.

I spent a year in my first job which ended when my employers' daughter moved in to care for them. I then worked for a year as a cook-housekeeper to a gentleman with a teenage son and daughter. When I left that job I worked and lived-in with the Kazmir family who owned a dress shop in Bournemouth. His uncle owned one in Southampton. I was the cleaner and nursemaid to the baby. The Kazmirs were Jewish and very particular about the way their food was cooked, so that was the job of Mrs Kazmir, though I did a few chores in the kitchen. Oh, how I missed bacon! On my day off I would go to the local café and have a bacon sandwich.

The Kazmir family were very kind to me and gave me clothes from their shop at Christmas or for my birthday. I had a large room of my own and all my food was included in my pay. Mrs Kazmir had a new-born baby, so I also learnt how to care for babies. Importantly, I bought a second-hand sewing machine and started to make my own clothes, though my time was mostly filled caring for the baby and doing all the housework. This was the bane of my life because I was told to thoroughly clean a room a day which meant moving all the furniture, and even cleaning the chandeliers. Every time the baby cried I had to see to him because Mrs Kazmir was often in the shop which was separate from the house.

I had visited my parents in 1947 and went again in 1949, 1951 and in 1953 just after I got married. Things had started to improve for my parents around 1949 and they were able to move to slightly better accommodation where they stayed for three or four years and from where Helli started school. From there they moved to Munnerstadt where again they lived on the upper floor of a farmhouse, but had three rooms plus a kitchen. It was around this time that my parents asked me to come back to live with them. I felt I was at a cross-roads in my life. Although I wanted to be with them I had a much better life in Bournemouth. I didn't want to share a bedroom and I didn't want to be living on an isolated farm where my prospects for work would be very limited. Eventually, I think they understood this but it caused them, and myself, a great deal of sadness.

I met my first boyfriend, Johnny, at the All Nations Club in Bournemouth. Our relationship was good until one day I fell out of his car, rolled down a bank and damaged my face quite badly. I felt very upset when I later learnt that he knew the catch of the passenger door was faulty, so falling from his car meant I fell out with him!

At the age of twenty-three I met my husband, Ronald Brooke, at the All Nations Club. He was a Yorkshireman who was working on a farm in Dorset, having just come back from New Zealand where he had moved after being demobbed from the Royal Air Force. He had been specially trained in Israel as a cinematographer and had run cinemas for the Forces. From Israel he was able to join a train which was returning Australians and New Zealanders to their homelands after the War. He did various jobs on farms and fruit factories in Australia and New Zealand and he also learnt to fly. On returning to England he had no reason to go back to Yorkshire, for his parents had both died and he was an only child.

At the All Nations Club I had become quite a good badminton player. Ronald was too, so we teamed up and thereafter he started to come to see me on my day off. It was a whirlwind romance because we met and got married within a month! We married on the 31st October 1953 and rented a flatlet in Wimborne, so obviously my job with the Kazmir family ended. Auntie Frieda and Charles and

his girlfriend Mary, whom he later married, came to our wedding and they organised a nice little reception for us at their home.

Erika Jenne and Ronald Brooke, wedding day in Bournemouth, 31 October 1953.

At this time Ron got a job in flight refuelling at a small airstrip just outside Wimborne and I got my first sewing job at a factory at the same location. I made candlewick bedspreads which were the height of fashion in the fifties. We travelled to work on his staff bus and from then on started to save money. Ron had been, and continued to be, very good at saving, and by that time my parents no longer needed me to send them money. I had an ambition to own our own home, whereas Ron had been accustomed to renting or living in a 'tied' house such as his parents did when working in the cotton mills in Yorkshire. I had to persuade him that buying was a very good option. In October 1954 we moved into our own brand new three bedroomed bungalow at 25 Ivor Road, Corfe Mullen. The land cost £150 and the bungalow cost £1,500 to be built. Our mortgage was nineteen pounds and sixpence a month.

Ron was earning ten pounds a week and I brought home up to six pounds a week if I worked overtime. We had very little furniture and slept on a mattress given to us by a neighbour. It took us another year or two before we were able to buy nice furniture, but this didn't worry me because we had a roof over our heads which was ours!

In 1955 my mother made her first trip to England bringing my little sister, Helli, who was ten years old. Sadly, my father felt he was too old to travel. We had a lovely reunion and my mother met Ron for the first time. She was so proud that we owned our own home and it was rather special for my mother to be with her two sisters, Auntie Annie and Auntie Frieda.

Mother's first visit to Bournemouth 1955. Left to right; Auntie Frieda, Mary (Charles' wife) and Auntie Annie behind.

Left to Right; Mother, Auntie Frieda, Charles, Ronald, Erika, Helli in front. Mother and Helli's visit to Bournemouth 1959.

Ron and I worked hard but we also played hard in that we cycled a lot and toured the country and coastal roads. We were both very fit and took up kayaking in Poole Harbour or on the Wimborne River. Ron also continued flying and often flew me on jaunts to the Isle of Wight. He wanted me to learn, but I didn't

have enough courage. It was almost nine years before we had our first child, a daughter. Prior to that I had had three miscarriages, all boys. Tania was born in February 1962 and I did get to notice that Ron was quite jealous of the time I was spending with the baby. As an only child he was not used to sharing attention or to taking second-place. Things eased a bit when Kim was born in November 1964 because Tania was by then getting to an interesting age and becoming a 'Daddy's girl'. They were happy days bringing up my girls – very happy days. I even took them by train to Germany for my father's eightieth birthday in 1966, where we had a wonderful family reunion. Ron wouldn't come and never did. He really didn't want me to go and was annoyed at having to look after himself whilst I was away.

Erika in light aircraft flown by Ronald. Dorset, early 1960s.

Auntie Frieda, Mother and Auntie Annie at Corfe Mullen, 1960s.

Sewing and dressmaking became an important part of my life once I had my babies. I used to go to jumble sales to buy second-hand dresses, material or coats, and would then cut them down to make other garments – just as I had seen being done when I was a child. I became quite proficient, and when my friends and neighbours saw the pretty things that my girls were wearing they asked me to make garments for their children too. When I got a request for more complicated garments then I would purchase a pattern, so my skills were widening and I was contributing more to the family finances.

Tania and Kim loved school and especially sports. They played tennis, badminton, did running and high-jump. They both passed their 'Eleven Plus'. Tania got a place at Queen Elizabeth Grammar School, Wimborne and Kim went to Corfe Hills School. Ron and I took the children on holiday to Wales where we all did canoeing, sailing and pony-trekking. By then we had a van which we would pile up with our girls, and sometimes their friends, and we would tour all the various beautiful sites

and beaches that we have down here on this coast. We loved Durdle Door, Lulworth Cove, Weymouth and Portland. The beaches of Sandbanks and Studland Bay were on our doorstep. We had beautiful times. Yes, they were definitely happy years.

However, as our girls grew older they developed minds of their own, which did not please my husband, and we started having arguments about this. The last few years of our marriage were not happy and I actually left him in August 1980. I initially stayed with my good friend, Rene Hearn, who lived close-by, and then I rented a flat in Wimborne. Kim was visiting my sister in Germany at the time, so Helli was able to help me break the news to her and she took it quite well. She had probably noticed that her father and I weren't living harmoniously.

Tania with Kim, 1967 (Tania's fifth birthday).

Tania did not complete her education but left school in 1978 aged sixteen after she met a boyfriend, John Faldo, when on holiday in Cornwall. Because she was in love, education sadly went out of her head! John lived on the Isle of Wight, so Tania wanted to move there too, which she did, taking a job as a receptionist at a holiday camp. John and Tania eventually both came to live in Bournemouth and got married here in 1981. I made the bride's and bridesmaids' dresses and her father begrudgingly gave her away. Their son, Stephen, was born in 1989.

Kim was doing very well academically and the school brought it to my attention that she was university material. She was encouraged by an amazing teacher called Sue Milbank who said she had nothing to lose in applying for a place at King's College, Cambridge University, no less. It was Sue Milbank, now Sue Calvert, who suggested that my life-story was worth telling. I was 'over the moon' and felt so proud

when she actually got a place. Kim visited her father to tell him but he wasn't at all interested. She studied Anthropology, Social and Political Studies, with Greek and Russian, although she later gave up the languages. I was even more delighted when, in 1986, her MA degree was awarded with First Class Honours. Kim kept in touch with her boyfriend Tim Evison throughout her university days, and they eventually married in 1990. Again I made all the dresses but her father did not give her away because she did not wish that.

In 1981 I met a man called Dave Owens who was younger than me but we got on really well. He came to Bournemouth from Bedford and was a friend of Rene's husband. After Kim left home to go to Cambridge University Dave moved in with me and we had a lovely life, though we were both working hard. I eventually received half of the money that my husband got for the bungalow but I had a loan to pay off which I had extended to help Kim at university. This left me with just £14,000 so I couldn't afford to buy a home in a costly place like Wimborne. After an extended search I eventually found this house in Emerson Road, Poole. It needed renovating, so I managed to buy it for £16,000. I didn't have any money for renovations so I returned to my frugal ways and saved, worked and saved. It was two-and-a-half years before the slow renovation of my house was complete, a process which I personally managed and took part in. In November 1985 I was able to move in. I had taken three jobs. I was doing sewing alterations for a dry cleaning shop in Wimborne, plus alterations for the dress shop called Country Classics. At the same time I was getting private referrals to make wedding dresses and ball gowns. In addition to that I got a job in the Sewing Room at Poole General Hospital. I absolutely loved that job because it was 'community' work and worthwhile. Nurses came to me for uniforms to be fitted, doctors came for their white coats, and I did repairs to bedding and made curtains for ward screens. Eventually I became the Supervisor of the Sewing Room. I met so many nice people and worked there for ten years before I retired in 1995, though I continued with my private sewing jobs for another five years.

Dave and I lived here together for almost three years before we split up. We had been together for around six years, during which we had some nice times, including holidays to Cornwall, Spain and even to Germany to see my family. We parted good company. Rene and I continued our companionship until she developed Alzheimer's disease. We had holidays together in Spain, Jersey, Egypt, Goa and even Germany. Rene's husband wasn't interested in travel. We ran a market stall at Wimborne Market selling garments I had made, we visited the theatre, or met up with other friends, and generally had a nice time in our retirement.

Today, Kim and Tim have two children, Ben and Claudia, and live in Easthope, Shropshire. Coincidentally, they live in the next village to Coalbrookdale where Mr Aston-Nicholas was born and brought up. Tania's son Steve and

his Polish wife, Renate, live in Lawford Dale, Manningtree, and Tania also lives in Essex, at Thorrington, with her partner, Tony Sharples. They all seem very happy. I have a lovely family, both here and in Bavaria, and feel very blessed.

Erika on holiday in Goa with her friend Rene Hearn.

Erika with her grandchildren, Steve standing, Ben and Claudia. In Erika's garden in Poole, Dorset. Erika's 70th birthday, 2000.

Erika with her daughters, Tania and Kim, on a cruise to Norwegian Fjords, 2010. Erika's 80th birthday.

My little sister, Helli, grew up fast and became a hairdresser. She married Dieter Mansius. Dieter came from the town of Vacha which was in the Communist zone of East Germany. In late August 1961, at the age of twenty-two, he made a courageous escape over the Berlin Wall, though it was actually the part that was bordering the River Werra. There was a terrific storm running that night so there was high water and the Communist border-guards with their guns were tucked inside their look-out towers taking refuge. Dieter braved the storm and in the darkness he swam across the fast-flowing river. The local West Germans he approached on the other side were friendly and took him in. They gave him dry clothes but warned he must leave within twenty-four hours because when the guards suspected someone had escaped they had a habit of crossing the river and searching the houses close-by. If they found a fugitive, they punished anyone who had given assistance, even though they were living outside their Communist zone. Dieter then walked for about fifty kilometres west-wards to stay with his older sister, Hannilore who happened to be living in the West. As good fortune would have it, her partner was an expert carpenter who made wooden floors and wood panelling. Dieter learnt the trade from him and he was eventually able to run his own very successful business. It was just luck that Helli ever met Dieter, you could say. After our father died in 1967, our widowed mother was cared for by them until she died in 1968 at the young age of sixty-three. Helli and Dieter now live in Oberwern near Schweinfurt. They had two children, Rainer and Sandra, and now have four grandchildren. We try to see one another at least once a year and we are in constant contact by telephone. My brother Walter has now passed away. He remained in the Essen area all his life and had two marriages. He had one daughter, Barbara, who had no children. She hasn't kept in touch recently. For the last years of his life Walter lived alone in a cottage in the woods, which he loved.

I have kept in touch with all my family in Bavaria though I only saw Karl once after the War. Living in the Communist-controlled zone of East Germany meant he was unable to leave, though he did make the one visit to Bavaria. He came with one of his sons, but as a guarantee of his return he had to leave his wife and other son behind. By 1989, when the control by Russia had ended, Karl had sadly died.

Uncle Joe, wife Rosa, Mother, Father, Dieter, Helli holding baby son Rainer, pregnant with Sandra, Bavaria, 1966.

Erika, Walter and Helli at the wedding of Barbara, Walter's daughter, Dusseldorf, near Essen, Germany, 1996.

Erika and Helli visiting Ceské Budějovice, 1989.

110

In 1989 I paid a pilgrimage to my little village of Rudolfov. Russia had collapsed and with it their dominance of Eastern Europe, including the fall of the Berlin Wall. I visited with my sister Helli, her husband, Dieter and my cousin Ignatz and his wife, Hannilore. Driving through the land everything seemed so run-down and buildings had been left dilapidated. Our old house looked so small in comparison to the way I remembered it. I knocked the door but the Czech lady who answered didn't take kindly to a stranger, so we didn't get to go inside. I visited again in 2005 with Kim and Tim, and in 2013 with my grandson, Steve, his wife Renate, and Helli and Deiter.

Auntie Annie remained as Mrs Aston-Nicholas and never remarried. She seemed to know a lot of people, including quite a few in the local Naturist Society, of which she was a member. Her Bohemian culture did not change a lot! She remained eccentric, becoming more so as she grew older. None of the family were particularly close to her because she was rather domineering and not at all motherly, unlike her brothers and sisters. She moved from White Gables and rented a flat in Michelgrove Road, Boscombe, in the early 1960s. Later White Gables was demolished to make way for a block of flats which was named Balmoral Court. Auntie Annie retained her old car which we could always hear approaching. Cats became her passion and she kept around twenty or more! She eventually moved to an old people's home but died six months later in a nursing home in Bournemouth. This was in 1997 when she was aged eighty-eight. I am so pleased that I retrieved the two painted plates from her few belongings after she died because, without these, we might not have known the story of Arthur Vincent Aston-Nicholas. Like a true professional, he painted his name and date on the back of these plates.

Erika with Auntie Annie Aston-Nicholas in nursing home. Bournemouth, 1997.

After the sixty-nine years that I have lived here I definitely feel English. In fact, it didn't take me long to feel English as I always got on well with the people and loved the English sense of humour. I felt happy, safe and free to express my opinions. I would have loved to have had the opportunity to study when I was younger, particularly languages and art, but my husband didn't agree with the idea, and thereafter I needed to earn money. Nevertheless, I feel I have had a good life and have the most lovely daughters and grandchildren. I am grateful to Auntie Annie but I feel more indebted to Mr Arthur Vincent Aston-Nicholas — a man I knew almost nothing about until the writing of this book.

SECTION THREE
JOHN DONNARUMMA RICHARDSON'S STORY

CHAPTER ONE
EARLY LIFE

I WAS BORN, JOHN Donnarumma, on the 17th November 1933 to Clotilda Assunta Donnarumma, known as Goodie, at 'St Elmo' Junction Road, Totton near Southampton. This was a house where unmarried girls went to give birth to their illegitimate off-spring. My mother was 'sweet twenty-one'. I didn't know who my father was. When I met my mother at the age of almost eleven she never spoke about him and never did from then on. However, my grandmother's niece, Rosina Esposito, aged ninety-four

and living in London, only recently told the author of this book she thought his name was Giovanni Carrani, a name she didn't know the spelling of – so perhaps I am a full-blooded Italian after all!

My first memories are from around the age of three when I was living with my grandmother, Trofimena Proto Donnarumma, whom I called 'Nanny', in Minori on the Amalfi

John Donnarumma aged about eight months, 1934.

John with his grandmother. In Minori, southern Italy, 1935.

Coast of southern Italy. According to documentation I recently acquired, I was baptised in Minori so I assume I lived there for the first five years of my life. I do recall the warmth and affection under the care of Nanny, whom I thought was my real mother. Also living with us was my cousin, Mario Donnarumma, later known as Tony, who was two years older than me though I can't recall much about him being there. His mother was Nanny's eldest daughter, Eleanora Donnarumma, known as Yana, who, like my mother, was also living and working in England.

Trofimena Proto Donnarumma with her grandsons, John on left, Mario (Tony) on right. Minori 1935.

All I can remember about my Nanny's home were the steps leading up to a sort of veranda garden with steps on the other side going down. I vaguely remember Italian relatives and friends coming to see my grandmother though I definitely remember Nanny's third son, my Uncle Dominic, and her youngest son Francesco, known as Uncle Babe, coming from England and spending time with us. I remember being rescued when I fell into a type of brazier burner used in winter to heat the inside of my Nanny's apartment. It was like a big, open copper dish which was fed with charcoal until it turned red hot. I can remember my Uncle Dominic snatching me up and plastering my bottom with butter to relieve the pain. Apparently, that's the worst way to treat a burn, though he did have the best intentions in mind. My Nanny couldn't read nor write Italian and only spoke pidgin English in a sort of slang way. Consequently, I only spoke Italian and didn't learn English until I was over five years old. When I went back to Minori many years after I had left, I found very few people in a place like Minori who could speak English.

Minori at the turn of the twentieth century. Collection of Maurizio Apicella.

The next memory I have is of coming back to England on a boat. I remember having a little toy car, or something similar, and for some reason I threw it into the water and a kindly seaman scooped it out with a bucket. This must have been at the beginning of 1939, or perhaps the summer of 1938, when there was dissension and general unrest in Italy and most of Europe, caused by a certain Mr Hitler. This probably prompted my grandmother to return Tony and myself to England where she felt we might be safer because we were English-born. She also probably wanted us to have an English education.

114

Trofimena with her grandsons, John, and Tony on right. Italian passport document used to return to England from Minori, 1938.

I can vaguely remember living close to Tudor House Museum in the Old Southampton area. I attended St Joseph's Roman Catholic School nearby. The form of punishment at St Joseph's was a thin cane on the back of the hand which seemed very painful. All I had done was to pinch a sweet from a bag that had been confiscated from another child by the nun who was teaching us. It seemed an easy ploy because I was sitting in the front row of the class, so that I could be taught to speak English, no doubt. Other memories are of street vendors selling peanuts and ice cream from carts made from bicycles with wooden boxes on the front. Another memory I have is watching with Nanny from a window above a shop or apartment in Bernard Street or Oxford Street and looking down on a Royal Procession progressing along the street from the Docks area. I think it was the King and Queen. Everybody was cheering.

King George VI and Queen Elizabeth arrived at Southampton Docks returning from their Royal Tour of Canada and North America on the ship 'The Empress of Canada' on 22 June 1939. They then toured through Southampton.

I can only just about remember my grandparents' Ice Cream Parlour in Canal Walk, so I must have been taken there. Nanny wasn't living there at that time but I can remember my Auntie Emily being there. I can't remember ever meeting my mother at that time.

John's mother, Goodie, c.1927. Ice Cream Parlour, Southampton.

Goodie (Clotilda) and Yana (Eleanora) Donnarumma. Canal Walk, c.1928.

My grandmother had seven children, all born in Southampton and at the time, all still living there. Three of her children, Nicolo, Carlo and Yana were married. Her other four children, Domenic, Clotilda known as Goodie, who was my mother, Amalia known as Emily, and

Francesco known as 'Babe', were living nearby or with their father, Achille Donnarumma, from whom my grandmother was separated – not that I knew many of these facts until much later in my life.

My Auntie Yana married a merchant seaman called Eddie Peden in 1933 and Mena was born in 1934, then Eddie in 1936, so I had two more cousins and Tony had a half-brother and sister. I loved being with my cousins, Tony, Mena and Eddie, and I was very close to my Auntie Yana who was very kind to me. I loved going to my Auntie Yana's home which was in Portswood Road. It had a long front garden with welcoming steps to the door. It was in this house at Portswood that I remember my grandmother talking about going back to Minori and wanting to take me with her. I remember kicking up a fuss and crying because I didn't want to go. I just wanted to stay with my cousins. War was looming and my grandmother did not have British citizenship. I realise now that, as an Italian subject living near a port, had she stayed in England she would have been interned as an 'Enemy Alien' in 1940 when Italy joined the War supporting

Trofimena Proto Donnarumma with her seven children, left to right, Nicolo, Carlo, Domenic, Eleanora (Yana), Clotilda (Goodie), Amalia (Emily) and Francesco (Baba or Francis). c.1926. Southampton.

116

the German Fascists. So Nanny did return to Minori, leaving me for a short time with my Auntie Yana and Uncle Ted. I remember I shared a bed with Tony. He slept one end of the bed and I slept at the other. I used to get a lot of nosebleeds, waking to find the pillow was red. Auntie Yana would always come with a handkerchief to help me. I felt she was my mother now.

Goodie with brother, Carlo, and a friend sitting. Outside Ice Cream Parlour, Canal Walk, c.1928.

Trofimena with her daughters Yana, Goodie and Emily. Canal Walk, c.1925.

Emily and Goodie with two Officers from Marconi's yacht, Southampton c.1932.

John's maternal grandparents were Achille Donnarumma, born 1880, and Trofimena Proto, born 1879, in the small fishing town of Minori on the Amalfi Coast of southern Italy. They were married in Minori in 1905 and shortly after emigrated to England where they had seven children and lived in King Street, a very impoverished area of old Southampton. Initially Achille sold fruit and vegetables from a pony and trap. From around 1913 the couple were able to rent a small shop at number fourteen Canal Walk where they sold fruit, vegetables and a little of their own home made ice cream. Their lives were interrupted by the First World War when Achille left to serve in the Italian Army, leaving Trofimena to run the shop. However, by around 1923 they took the opportunity to acquire the building next door to them, number thirteen, the Horse Shoe Tavern, and they set about converting their shop and the tavern into one property – an ice cream parlour and refreshment rooms. This became enormously popular and very profitable, to the extent that Achille and Trofimena were able to purchase a many-roomed villa in Sorrento, close to Minori. They let the building as seven apartments but intended to reside there in retirement. In the meantime the couple made many sojourns to the place of their birth.

In the late 1920s Achille and Trofimena's marriage came under strain when Achille began to have affairs with younger women. Trofimena therefore spent more time in Minori or stayed with one of her adult daughters in Southampton. In 1938 Achille renamed the Ice Cream Parlour as D'Orsay Refreshment Rooms after his twenty-four year old lover, Loise Violet D'Orsay, also known as Dyer. Domestic bliss was not however to be his for long, for in May 1939, at the age of fifty-nine, he died from a heart attack whilst staying with Loise in a hotel in London. In his Will Achille bequeathed the refreshment rooms to Loise. Achille's wife and children were disinherited, apart from Emily who was granted ten shillings a week. Six months later Loise married a seaman, Mr Harry Murphy, in the parish church of All Saints. The marriage was short-lived and replaced with a long-term relationship with a well-known Southampton garage proprietor, Richard Baker. This relationship was interrupted by a short marriage to his manager, Gerald Goodbody. In 1964 Loise' disturbed life ended in tragedy when she took an overdose of alcohol and barbiturates. The ice cream parlour and refreshment rooms were bombed during the Second World War. At the end of the War the land was cleared and compulsorily purchased for new building. This was the end of an era.

Throughout the Second World War Trofimena Proto Donnarumma lived in her home village of Minori where she was eventually interned because her English-born children were in the British Forces. When the Germans were defeated by the Americans and other Allies at the Battle of Salerno in September 1943, Trofimena's eldest son, Nicolo, was able to secure her release since his British regiment happened to be part of the invading Allied victors. She was in a frail and starving state so he brought her food from his Army rations. An article in a local Southampton newspaper reported: "In war brother meets brother but seldom a son meeting his mother".

CHAPTER TWO
MISERERE NOBIS – NAZARETH HOUSE,
WAR BEGINS, EVACUATION TO WARDOUR CASTLE

MY SCHOOL WAS SUDDENLY changed to Springhill Primary in Hill Lane which was a Roman Catholic school right next to Nazareth House orphanage for boys, which was also Roman Catholic. From documentation I recently obtained, my mother had made a personal application to the nuns, the Sisters of Nazareth, requesting them to accept me into their orphanage, the two reasons being that my grandmother was returning to Italy and couldn't take me with her, and my mother was a servant in Brighton. I don't remember who took me to Nazareth House. Perhaps it was my mother who would have been a stranger to me, but on the 4th July 1939 I was admitted there. I remember being told I was going there and I thought it might be a new adventure. I also assumed I would still see my cousins and aunts. I can't recall being distressed, and even at my young age I was able to appreciate the sense of peace and tranquillity, the beautiful walled garden, the statues and the huge wooden cross on which was nailed a figure of Christ.

I don't remember much about Nazareth House because I was only there for a couple of months before I was evacuated due to the threat of bombing in the War that had just begun. I do remember about a dozen boys practising on various brass instruments but for some unknown reason, once we were evacuated, the band never functioned again. I thought that a pity because they were good. The last memories I have of Nazareth House are its shiny floors, the smell of polish, and that it was spotlessly clean.

On the 2nd September 1939, the morning following Britain's declaration of War with Germany, two double-decker buses and a lorry arrived outside Nazareth House to take aboard eighty-four children from the ages of one to twelve, together with beds and bedding. We set off amidst an air of great excitement and jubilation. The sky was filled with barrage

Nazareth House, Hill Lane, Southampton, c.1923. Bombed in the Second World War, not rebuilt until 1953.

balloons for as far as the eye could see, gradually thinning as we left the vicinity. In what seemed no time at all we arrived at Wardour Castle in Wiltshire, which is just past Salisbury, and near to the small village of Tisbury. The 'castle' was huge and almost crescent-shaped. It appeared bleak and sombre, reminiscent of Satis House in Dickens' *Great Expectations*. At one end was a small chapel and the main part of the building was where the owner's family lived. The other end on the left, the east wing, had been loaned to the Sisters of Nazareth to accommodate the orphan children from Nazareth House. This end of the house was unkempt and void of electricity. Due to the limited accommodation, it was decided to transfer forty infants aged under six to Nazareth House in Swansea, which left forty-four boys under the care of five or six nuns at Wardour.

Wardour Castle was the stately home of Lord Gerald and Lady Ivy Arundell. Lady Arundell was a devout Roman Catholic who offered the unused and neglected East Wing of her large home to the Sisters of Nazareth from the orphanage in Southampton to accommodate wartime child evacuees. She was particularly happy to accommodate the forty-four boys although she had little contact with them and they were forbidden to venture into the main building, the West Wing or gardens. The only view the boys had of Lady Arundell was when she attended All Saints Chapel which adjoined the West Wing of the house. She would wear a black lace face veil and pray from the balconies of the church which she accessed directly from her home.

Our excitement with the evacuation was short-lived however, as the nuns exerted their authority with an arm of iron. Religion predominated our lives. We had to attend twice daily church services, Mass in the mornings and Angelus in the evenings, as well as eight or nine prayer sessions per day and three church services on Sundays. Father Flynn or Father Walsh would conduct the services. The younger priests were a bit sadistic and used to perform silly tricks with lighted cigarettes on the palms of our hands. The principal subject at school was, naturally, Religious Study, at which I excelled. I enjoyed the peace and quiet, the hymn

Wardour Castle taken in 1934 by trainee pilots flying out of Old Sarum Airfield, Salisbury. East Wing on left accommodated the Nazareth House boys, Chapel on right, at front of West Wing. Courtesy of Mr Barry Williamson.

singing, the smell of incense and the many services, mostly in Latin, for which I seemed to have an affinity — but in spite of all the brain-washing I was in two minds, as part of me wanted to respond and the other to rebel. I was easily captivated by the charisma and the adornment of the church. It seemed a beautiful religion in that it sought to promote a civilised way of life but it seemed flawed because of its contradictions and hypocrisy. Fear was used as a tool to intimidate us. We were told that if we died whilst committing a mortal sin we would burn in Hell for all eternity, whilst a venal sin would condemn us to a spell in Purgatory. An example of mortal sin would be to omit keeping holy the Sabbath without just cause. Hell was a surface of fire — so we were naturally frightened.

The nuns exercised strict discipline. We soon discovered that the ones to watch out for were those under the influence of the head nun, Sister Ann, who turned out to be a raving psychopathic nut, better suited to confinement in an asylum than to the charge of young children. Punishment for the least misdemeanour was usually a sound thrashing with a heavy stick which was used with such relish and force that it would sometimes break in two. After bedtime Sister Ann would often walk the dormitories in silent prayer, being the pious lady she was, and if she detected the slightest movement from any bed, indicating that the occupant was still awake or doing rude things, the stick would come crashing down across the bed with some ferocity. Not a word was spoken as she moved on in search of her next victim. Strangely, there were times when Sister Ann showed a different face, one that was genteel and kind, especially towards a certain sweet-looking child whom she treated as a pet, but being aware of her ways, we always approached her with caution and trepidation.

We slept in three dormitories grouped in ages. There were metal single beds with sheets and a blanket. I was always terrified of soiling the sheets so I never used them. I used to keep them folded and go to bed with just a blanket. Around nine o'clock every night we were roused and made to urinate in a bucket. It was supposed to stop bed-wetting but it didn't always work. One night, after being roused, I got back into another boy's bed by mistake, as I was still half asleep. The nuns must have thought I was intent on carnal gratification because I was given a sound thrashing, as was the boy into whose bed I had ventured — I was just seven years old! I remember if a boy wet the bed his face was rubbed in the wet bedding, he was made to strip and get into a cold bath, his head was submerged for several seconds then he was doused with bucket after bucket of icy cold water. One brave soul who had the temerity to call Sister Ann 'a pig' was made to don a loin cloth and crawl on his hands and knees a dozen times round the recreation room, in front of all the boys, chanting "I am a pig, I am a pig" before being allowed to dress again. I remember when one boy messed in his bed he was made to stand holding his faeces in his hands at breakfast. Sister Ann told him that if he wanted some breakfast he could eat what he was holding!

I recall sleep-walking quite a lot. The first time I suspected I had been sleep-walking was on waking up one morning and finding my hands and feet were blackened as though I had been up a chimney, evidence of which was confirmed at a later time when I woke up and found myself in the cellars. As I made my way back along the darkened corridors I bumped into a nun. "Who's that?" she gasped. I just scooted back to my dormitory as fast as my little legs would carry me. Thank goodness the place had no electricity. I wondered later if the nun might have thought she'd encountered a ghost because I heard no more of the incident. I never mentioned my sleep-walking to another soul and I imagine other boys similarly afflicted did not, or they may not have been aware that they were sleep-walkers.

The lack of electricity meant the only form of lighting was by candles or paraffin lamps and the only heating was an open fire in the recreation room. As the nuns' quarters were strictly out of bounds there was no way of knowing if they enjoyed the comfort of open fires. I knew there was a way of heating water because, on rare occasions, the Saturday morning weekly bath was unbearably hot, though most of the time, even in winter, we suffered cold baths. The two baths lay back to back in partitioned rooms which were each large enough to accommodate four boys side by side in a kneeling position. On emerging we had to undergo a cleanliness inspection which meant a clout on the head and a second bath if we didn't come up to muster.

Every fortnight we were treated to a head bath which was generally given in the dining room after supper. A tin bath was filled with hot water and a liberal amount of Jeyes Fluid was added. Jeyes Fluid was, and still is, a stringent disinfectant outdoor cleaner. We all lined up to have our heads submerged in this solution. Our heads were then scrubbed with carbolic soap, the idea being to eliminate head lice and other 'nasties' lurking in the hair. The result was stinging eyes, throbbing heads and faces covered in red blotches.

There were just two toilets in the East Wing of Wardour Castle so an outdoor portable loo had to be constructed to facilitate the needs of forty-four boys. The several-seater structure was placed on top of a trench dug by the older boys. There were no partitions or doors and we used grass or dock leaves to wipe our bottoms. When the trench was full it was in-filled with lime and earth and the loo moved to a freshly-dug trench. In summertime the place stank to high heaven and in winter it was freezing. I remember a boy falling into the stinking excrement. A cold bath and beating followed.

I can only recall one visit from a dentist in all the time I spent at Wardour Castle. The day before he was due a single toothbrush was produced, charged with toothpaste, and given to the first boy to use. He then spat out into a bucket of water, rinsed the brush in the same water then passed the toothbrush to the next boy. Never once was the bucket emptied and refilled. The last boy to use it felt very sick.

Incessant thirst during the summer was another problem hard to accept because we were denied access to the bathroom during the day. To slake our thirst we resorted to drinking from ponds and streams when out walking. Only the most courageous and foolhardy would sneak to the bathroom. I was almost caught on one occasion. Luckily I had closed the door to the partitioned bath and was just about to take a drink when a nun came in and relieved herself. I held my breath and froze and my heart went into overdrive. The nun flushed the toilet and left and in my fear I forgot to take a drink. For weeks after that I had nightmares of the consequences had I been caught, the seriousness of the crime being compounded by the fact that a boy had actually witnessed a nun having a pee! I'm sure that if I had died at that moment my soul would have been cast into the Fires of Hell for all eternity. 'Agnes Dei qui tolis peccata mundi, miserere nobis!' (Lamb of God who takest away the sins of the World, have mercy on us).

Brian Osborne, from Nazareth House, as a choir boy at All Saints Chapel, Wardour, 1942. Courtesy of Mr Brian Osborne.

The nuns used to cook the food and it was awful. Breakfast was always the same; lumpy porridge without sugar, a slice of bread spread with dripping, and a mug of unsweetened cocoa. The reason given for the frugal midday and evening meals, which were often a type of stew followed by sago or semolina pudding, was that there was rationing due to the War. However, we weren't blind to the fact that the Sisters of Nazareth were well nourished. On one occasion we saw inside the pantry when its usually locked door was left open. Inside, stacked from floor to ceiling, was every conceivable type of tinned food. A couple of boys dared to take some and it wasn't missed. I don't know how they opened the tins! Before bed, we were given bread spread with margarine, which we called 'bread and scrape', together with a mug of milk which was sometimes rancid. One day we were given a 'treat' of cake instead of bread though it must have been stale or rotten because I was violently sick. It was subsequently assumed by the nuns that greed was to blame for my vomiting and consequently I was punished by a beating; a double whammy!

All boys below the age of twelve were marched the mile to Wardour Primary School which I liked very much because it afforded some respite from the hardship of Wardour Castle. The school was mostly run by a different Order of nuns called 'The Sisters of Mercy', nicknamed the 'butterfly nuns' because of the shape of their headgear. These nuns were kind and gentle and in particular I remember a Sister Lucy who had a table tennis bat which she called 'the Derby' with which she intended to administer corporal punishment, though she never really used it.

Our march to school was always accompanied by two Sisters of Nazareth nuns. We didn't wear shoes, except on Sundays or in bad winter weather, so it was difficult to outpace the nuns, though when we did we were able to raid a vegetable garden or two, or scrump a few apples. Chestnuts and beechnuts were another source of nourishment when in season as well as some varieties of grasses. The nuns sometimes used to march us on walks at weekends or during the summer school holidays, often to Old Wardour Castle, but never into Tisbury village or to areas where we might meet any local people.

At school we were known as 'the Castle boys' and the local children didn't really mix well with us. We tended to feel awkward and shy in their presence. I can't remember having any food at school though we did have a small bottle of milk which we drank with a straw and which was warmed on the school stove. I liked school a great deal and got on well. Perhaps for this reason I became a sort of 'star pupil' or 'little pet'. I became particularly good at Maths and I had a good memory. I remember one year a Christmas pantomime was performed at the school and I was chosen to take part. I found this exciting and recall one of the songs we sang – 'We are the soldiers of the King, my lads' – wearing a tin soldier's uniform of a red braided tunic and feathered hat. For the formation dancing I was paired with a girl from Tisbury with whom I fell madly in love, although I never did know her name. The school had a Christmas raffle which I won by choosing the number twelve, after the twelve apostles. I felt I couldn't keep the prize of a box of little bricks which could be made into a picture so I gave it back to the Sister of Charity who gave it to another boy, which disappointed me because I thought it might be offered to me again at a later time.

In the school summer holidays we were given free time to play in an adjacent field to Wardour Castle. We were sometimes roasted by the hot sun and were always thirsty. We played with wooden hoops or made boats from sticks and string. We played leap frog or oranges and lemons or imitated shooting down enemy aircraft with pretend 'ack-ack' guns. However, there were always plenty of chores to be done. The older boys dug latrines or scrubbed floors and the younger boys cleaned shoes or darned socks, which I wasn't good at, so rather than face the wrath of Sister Ann, I would keep beside me a couple of socks properly darned by another boy ready for her inspection.

One event that stands out vividly in my memory was a balmy Sunday when Lady Arundell allowed the use of her beautiful garden for an open-air Mass in honour of The Blessed Virgin Mary, Queen of the May. Never before did we know what existed on the South and West sides of Wardour Castle as these areas were strictly out of bounds to us, but we were treated to a spectacular aura of fragrant and colourful flowers of every description. I was overwhelmed by the same feeling of calmness I had experienced on my entry into Nazareth House. I can remember word for word one of the hymns we sang:-

Bring flowers of the rarest

Bring blossoms of the fairest

From garden and woodland

And hillside and dale

Our full hearts are swelling

Our glad voices telling

The praise of the loveliest

Flowers of the vale

Mary we crown thee with blossoms today

Queen of the angels and Queen of the May

O Mary we crown thee with blossoms today

Queen of the angels and Queen of the May

Cocooned in our little safe haven we were blissfully unaware of the carnage and destruction taking place in the 'World at War' though we were treated one night to a practical demonstration when a sole German aircraft returning from a sortie off-loaded two bombs close-by. I missed the excitement because I slept right through it but the bombs formed two craters in the field which later filled with rainwater and froze in winter. One boy, who was a bit of a bully, fell through this ice and almost drowned because it took us so long to

rescue him. If we hadn't been there he would surely have drowned. We bore him no grudge! The British Army set up a transit camp of tents in the grounds of Wardour Castle but we had little contact with the soldiers. When the Americans arrived they offered us chocolate and sweets. They put on a party for us and every boy was allocated to a soldier. Mine was called Jo. Afterwards, Sister Ann collected most of the sweets from us and later proclaimed "I've got sweets here for the boys who handed in their sweets. No boy who I saw eating sweets will get any more." We were all too frightened to go forward and get more sweets!

All Saints Chapel, Wardour Castle. Lady Arundell would pray from the balconies above the altar. The doors adjoined her home.

Weekly confession had to be made to the priest on Sundays. We were told by the nuns that to have rude thoughts or do rude things was sinful, though they omitted to tell us what the rude things were. There is no finer tutor than nature to give instruction on the facts of life and the boys readily passed on their feelings to one another as a natural process of growing up. I never experienced nor witnessed any sexual abuse or homosexuality so I don't know if it happened or not. Sexual knowledge was gleaned by the passing of smutty jokes and anecdotes. My confession would usually be along these lines – "Bless me Father, for I have sinned. I have been having rude thoughts and have been doing rude things." I was never asked what these were but my penance would usually be "One Our Father, and three Hail Marys" for bad thoughts, and doubled for the rude deeds, fairing a lot better than what the nuns would have dished out!

The boys cried at night for emotional reasons though mostly because they had received corporal punishment. It would seem that nature stepped in with a helping hand to compensate for the hardship and cruelty we endured and we became hardened to the beatings. The psychological harm however, would take years to heal, but for some the damage was permanent. We bonded to form a mutual union of friendship and camaraderie such as seldom seen today. We generally looked out for one another and any disagreements which escalated to fisticuffs usually terminated with a handshake. I had many 'brothers' and can remember many of their names. I have recently been in touch with Brian Osborne, Larry Barnett and 'Skinny Ryan', now named John Savage.

Not all of the nuns at Wardour Castle were bossy, domineering and cruel. The head nun, Sister Ann and those under her influence were vicious and sadistic. Sister Bonabenture, Sister Peter and Sister Alphonse were more kind. Another person who was kind to us was a young girl called Mary Symonds who had been brought up in a Nazareth House for girls, quite possibly in Southsea, Portsmouth. She undertook general household tasks, laundry and cleaning and looked after the younger boys. She was always smiling and caring to us all, and that helped us prevent the nuns from totally breaking our spirits.

During the course of my research I met two other ex-residents of Nazareth House and Wardour Castle, Mr John Savage, now aged eighty-seven, once known as Michael Ryan or 'Skinny Ryan', and

Mr Brian Osborne, now aged eighty-one. I have also had telephone contact with Mr Larry Barnett who lives in California. He is also eighty-one.

The accounts of John Savage, Brian Osborne and Larry Barnett, in relation to the treatment they received in Nazareth House and Wardour Castle, are similar to John Donnarumma Richardson's. It appears that some boys were treated more sadistically than others, especially the older boys. Sister Ann had one 'pet' who would sit on her lap. He was a 'lovely-looking' little boy with curly hair.

Others who rebelled or spoke out, who wet or messed their beds, who vomited or even dropped a Bible, received harsh punishments as well as having their soiled sheets rubbed into their faces. Sister Ann was in charge and her favourite weapon was a sawn-off billiard cue. Marks on legs or heads were the norm. Pants down in front of the other boys and six whacks, or six strikes to each hand, resulted in swollen or bleeding buttocks or hands that didn't recover for a week or two. Other punishments included cold baths, withdrawal of food, standing in the corner with arms up, or kneeling on hard, dried peas.

Brian Osborne's older brother, Donald, constantly ran away from Wardour in an endeavour to reach his mother's home in Southampton. On each return to Wardour by the Police he was maliciously beaten. When it was felt that an extra harsh punishment was needed Sister Ann would request the handyman-carpenter of the Wardour Estate, Charlie Foyle, to carry out the beatings. Whilst a lot of boys did endure and recover from their treatment, some did not. Donald Osborne was one who did not. In adulthood he refused to acknowledge his existence at Nazareth House or Wardour Castle and would never discuss any aspect of it. He was initially successfully employed, married and had children, but the psychological trauma of his younger life lead to a disrupted life and his early death. Sister Ann, of the Presentation Morrison, became a professional nun in 1927. She died in her late eighties at Northampton Nazareth House in April, 1990.

CHAPTER THREE
RESCUE FROM PURGATORY

AFTER BREAKFAST ON THE morning of the 14th February 1944, Sister Ann came to tell me that my mother was coming today to take me away to live with her. Instead of going to school I was given a change of clothing and told to wait in the entrance for her arrival. I was overwhelmed with a feeling of such happiness that my mind went into a kind of euphoric stupor, yet I also felt great sorrow at leaving my friends, especially as I had not been given the chance to say goodbye to them. Despite the cruelty of the nuns and their misguided concepts I had been happy with my friends. I was ten-and-a-half years old and I had been

John's mother Goodie Donnarumma, surname now changed to Richardson in ATS uniform.

in the orphanage for almost five years. As a child five years seems more like fifty. I also had no recollection of having a mother.

At about ten o'clock my mother turned up accompanied by my Auntie Emily. They were both wearing ATS (Auxiliary Territorial Service) Army uniforms and I thought they looked lovely. I didn't recognise either of them. I was expecting to see my Italian grandmother whom I called Nanny. My mother introduced herself as Goodie and told me my aunt was called Emily. We were soon on the bus to Southampton and I was feeling like a convict who had served a life sentence suddenly being released on parole. I asked my mother why she hadn't written to me and she said she didn't want to make the other boys jealous!

I was now an 'ordinary' person, away from the orphanage, though I didn't feel very ordinary because I wasn't close to my mother. I tried to speak to her but she found it difficult to, well, love me. In fact, I felt she was a stranger, having rejected me from birth and making no contact whatsoever until she came to fetch me from comparative safety to one of imminent danger because the War was still raging, and there would still be nineteen months until its end. I later discovered the added disquieting fact that when she was conscripted into the ATS in 1942 only married mothers were exempt from military service. However, at the beginning of 1944 the ruling was changed to also allow unmarried mothers to become exempt, so she jumped at the chance to get out of the ATS by coming to claim me!

For a while we lived in a room in a house in Bernard Street, Southampton. The place was teeming with Services personnel and American soldiers. I know now that they would have been preparing for the invasion of the D-Day Landing

Beaches in Normandy. I did not meet up with my cousins, probably because they had been evacuated. My mother got a job as a waitress though we soon moved to Bournemouth and lived in an apartment above a hairdresser's shop which exuded a strong smell of ammonia. Bournemouth was also full with British and American soldiers. One of my mother's saving graces was that she was a superb cook who could turn the most basic foods into gastronomic delights and this talent rubbed off on me in later life. I felt awkward calling her 'Goodie' so I demanded that I call her 'Mum' which I did until she died even though I was to see little of her in my future life.

Mum organised for me to attend the Holy Cross School at Pokesdown which was Roman Catholic and run by nuns, but despite making new schoolmates I found it hard to adjust to a life of comparative ease, so I became surly and unruly. Instead of attending school I often walked to Poole to spend time at the boating lake. Most of the hotels around Bournemouth had been converted to billets for the American soldiers who turned out to be an easy touch for sweets or loose change. My greeting to my new-found friends was "Got any gum chum?" I'd invariably return home with my pockets full. I also became addicted to watching movie films and used to stand around outside the cinemas hoping that some American soldier with his girlfriend would allow me to accompany them into an adult-only 'A' film. An American soldier would often pay for me just to impress the girl with him. Surprisingly, by the time I left Holy Cross School I was considered to be a star pupil!

I also got attached to a Jewish gentleman who ran a little haberdashery shop. I used to go there at school dinner times and offer to look after his shop whilst he went to have his lunch. I used to take a couple of half-crowns from the till though I never spent the money but used to bury it or share it among school friends who would wait for me in an old bombed building site. I was eventually found out and soon after that we moved back to Southampton.

I really missed the boys at Wardour, so much so that my euphoria turned to dysphoria, so I hatched a plan to be with them again and persuaded two of my new school friends to join me in the venture. The idea was that we would live like hermits in the cellar of Wardour Castle. One morning, instead of going to school, I filled a large suitcase with all Mum's ill-gotten tinned foods, clothing and other essentials, and my friends arrived to help me hump the case to Boscombe Railway Station where we boarded the train to Tisbury, changing at Southampton and Salisbury. Surprisingly, we weren't challenged till we reached Tisbury when the Police were called because we didn't have any tickets. I do believe that my mother was less upset about her son going missing than she was about having her booty of tinned foods confiscated!

After about seven or eight months in Bournemouth my mother and Auntie Emily, who used to visit us regularly from Southampton, schemed a cunning plan together. My surname was changed to Robson which was Auntie Emily's name. A few weeks later Auntie Emily claimed release from the ATS stating that I was her son. When the deception failed she simply discharged herself and fled from Southampton to Bournemouth. I remember being in the kitchen when a Military Policeman from the Special Investigation Branch arrived and was talking with my mother and Auntie Emily in the sitting room. The next thing I knew was that Auntie Emily, who must have told the Policeman she was going to the toilet, came into the kitchen and told me to keep talking as though she was still with me. Whilst I talked she slipped out of the back door, down to the street and straight to Boscombe Railway Station. When the Policeman realised she had escaped he went flying down the steps in hot pursuit but he never found her. She sought refuge at the Horse and Groom public house in East Street, Southampton where she worked as a barmaid and called herself Sylvie. The Police pestered my mum and Auntie Yana for several months but eventually gave up searching for her. The Horse and Groom at that time was a notorious pub which was very popular with seamen, American GIs and 'ladies of the night'. There were two enormous stuffed brown bears in the bar and the staff were protected by iron bars on the counters, much like a bank. The drinks were passed through the bars! The pub was demolished in 1972.

The Horse and Groom public house in East Street, Southampton. Canal Walk to left in background.

It wasn't until the 27th February 1953 that an Amnesty was proclaimed to pardon all deserters of the British Forces as part of the Coronation celebrations, so Auntie Emily Robson, alias Sylvie, was able to come out of hiding and resume her role as a responsible member of society, complete with National Insurance Card and passport!

After that my mother decided to change our surname by Deed Poll to Richardson, which was my middle name. The teachers at my school must have been as confused and bewildered as I was to note my surname was Donnarumma, then Richardson, then Robson and back to Richardson in so short a time.

Mum worked as a waitress in a café owned by a Mr and Mrs Lawson. She also did her bit for the War effort by bringing American soldiers to our flat and she eventually struck up a longer relationship with an American GI called Jimmy who was friendly enough, but mostly indifferent towards me. Jimmy turned out to be a bit of a will-of-the-wisp. When the Second World War ended on 2nd September 1945 and he was sent back home, we never heard from him again. I never did know his surname.

Bournemouth beach was cleared of mines and the public allowed access but the barbed wire defences placed at low level tidemark remained in situ for some time as I found to my cost when I suffered a severe laceration that needed treatment.

In May 1946 my mother decided we should move back to Southampton. I was placed to live with my Auntie Yana and my cousins Tony, Mena, Eddie and Michael who had been born in 1942. Uncle Ted had adopted Tony in 1940. It was sheer heaven to feel a sense of belonging. It was the only time in my life I really felt I was part of a family. Auntie Yana was an excellent cook, even better than my mother. For a time I was returned to my original school of Springhill, a few yards from Nazareth House. At school I even met up with Brian Osborne, one of the boys from Wardour Castle.

John's cousins; Mena, Tony and Eddie Peden.

My bubble burst when Uncle Ted was demobbed from the Forces. He wasn't too happy to have acquired an extra child, so I had to pack my bags, and that broke my heart. I was inconsolable and felt my world had come to an end. I was moved eight doors away and taken in by a Mrs Miguel who was a jolly Danish lady of large proportions and her husband, George, who was a Portuguese merchant seaman. They had a daughter and two sons although just one son, Peter, was still living at home. I became quite fond of their dog, Monty, and as he was being rather neglected I had many an adventure with him. Food rationing was still in force and I was sent on many an errand or told to stand in a shop queue for many an hour.

My mother, or perhaps it was one of my aunts, must have noticed that I was quite bright because at the age of thirteen I was enrolled into an entrance exam at St Mary's College, Bitterne, Southampton which was a Roman Catholic Grammar School run by the Brothers of Christian Instruction. I passed and got a scholarship grant though my mother had to contribute eight pounds a term towards the fees. Although the school could boast a high level of success it was too little, too late for me. However, the emphasis of teaching leaned heavily towards religion so in any general exams my marks were highly boosted by the results I attained in Religious Studies. I had memorised all of the Mass services in Latin and could recite the Catechism from cover to cover, thanks to the Sisters of Nazareth at Wardour Castle! Apart from that I was good at chess, boxing and took part in several school plays.

John Donnarumma Richardson in St Mary's College uniform.

St Mary's College Southampton, 1947. John seated second row far left.

I was still missing my friends from Wardour Castle and several times I took bus journeys to see them. Since the War had finished the boys had been transferred from Wardour Castle to Melchet Court, a Jacobean style mansion in rural Sherfield English just outside Romsey, Hampshire. I remember the last time I visited them some of the boys were very excited about their imminent emigration to Australia or Canada. This would have been about 1946 or 1947. Over sixty-five years later, I now shudder to think that I might have been one of those child emigrants, many of whom were enslaved or sexually abused in those far off lands.

In 1948, at the age of fifteen, my mother said she could no longer afford the eight pounds a term towards my school fees so I left to face the world and all it had to offer. I passed my final exams and was awarded a Junior Oxford Certificate which I learnt later only qualified me for further Grammar School study. It was not until I joined the Army that I obtained the School Certificate.

In order to pay family debts, Wardour Castle was sold in 1947 to the Jesuits who, in 1961, sold it to Cranbourne Chase School for Girls. The school remained there until 1990. In 1992 Wardour was sold as a home to Mr Nigel Tuersley who spent millions of pounds renovating the interior to a truly spectacular standard. The East and West Wings were then developed into superior flats but the massive central building with its Great Hall was retained as an entire home and called 'The Apartment'. In 2010 this lovely main building was sold to the Conran family. The film 'Robin Hood, Prince of Thieves' was made there in 1991, as were scenes in the film 'Billy Elliot' in 2000. Wardour's lakes were used in the film 'Chocolat' in 2001. The Roman Catholic chapel is still functioning as part of the parish of The Sacred Heart, Tisbury, and All Saints, Wardour.

The Sisters of Nazareth ran their orphanage at Melchet Court from 1946 until 1954. They then returned to Nazareth House, Southampton following its extensive renovation due to the wartime bombing of November 1940. In the 1960s part of the building was used as a maternity wing for unmarried mothers, and in 1981 a new building for elderly residents was opened and named St. Basil's. The last boy left the house in August 1984. The building was finally closed at the end of May 2000 when the property was sold and demolished. In its place is a modern residential care home for the elderly named St. Basil's Christian Care Home.

CHAPTER FOUR
A WORKING LIFE

ON LEAVING SCHOOL MUM wanted me to train as a hairdresser but a short spell on virtually no wages with the Italian hairdresser, Ernie Spacagna, did not enthral me. My first proper job was as a junior shop assistant at G A Dunn and company, a gentlemen's outfitters and hat shop at 81 Above Bar, Southampton. I earned the princely wage of two pounds a week, plus commission, which averaged ten shillings – fifty pence today. It was a friendly place to work and I loved the shop's lovely oak panelling and large glass-fronted display window. On the negative side I had to wear a trilby hat when out and I had to put up with trying to eradicate the rats behind the walls when in. As a result of Hitler's bombing blitz of Southampton High Street many damaged beautiful Georgian and Victorian buildings were demolished after the War to make way for modern shops with tasteless facades. I noticed, even at my young age, that Councillors of the day had a lot to answer for.

At this time I was living with my Auntie Emily in Onslow Road. In 1946 Auntie Emily had unofficially fostered a child called Bruce Salak from an American GI bride en route to America. We believe she heard about baby Bruce in the Horse and Groom pub where she was a barmaid and kindly took him on. He was never officially adopted but he was another cousin for me, even though he was thirteen years younger. Bruce grew up to be very successful in his chosen profession. By this time my Auntie Emily was in what was to become a life-time relationship with Peter Groves who was then a merchant seaman, though they never had children.

After just over a year I got my second job. I was to become a cabin boy on the yacht called the 'Lutra' which was a converted motor

John in Cabin boy uniform on the yacht 'Lutra'.

torpedo boat owned by a Mr Portlock who was a retired managing director. The skipper, Mr Young and his son Andrew, an engineer, ran the yacht and I carried out cleaning, cooked breakfast, washed dishes and did deck work. I had no clue about boats but I had an impressive uniform! The yacht was newly painted and looked lovely. I joined the yacht in Wootton Creek on the Isle of Wight and we sailed to Amsterdam, Copenhagen, around the Swedish islands and as far as Denmark.

I thought these places were beautiful. I even visited Mrs Miguel's friend whom I called Auntie Denmark. However, I had to work for up to sixteen hours at a stretch, sometimes feeling quite seasick. I had some amusing experiences on the deck trying to avoid the yacht scraping its sides along the locks, or trying to prevent precious crystal glasses from being smashed by a falling fan. I had no idea how to row the small boat ashore and back, so I damaged that too. My breakfast cooking wasn't very good either and I noticed that the guests on board were throwing it over the side. By the time we returned to British waters I had not received any wages, and since it seemed as though I wasn't going to get any, on leaving the yacht I felt justified in packing my case with several bottles of whisky which I gave to my mother. Eventually, for six months' employment, working many hours, I received just twenty two pounds. However, despite all the negative factors, I had an experience I would not have wanted to miss. I never felt depressed or unhappy and I just marvelled at the wonderful and beautiful places we visited.

John off duty on the deck of the 'Lutra'.

At the age of seventeen I had the choice of undertaking my National Service or of joining the Army as a Regular. I chose the latter and signed up for a five-year duty with the Royal Army Dental Corps. Prior to that, having saved my twenty-two pounds hard-earned wages, I wanted to take the opportunity to visit my grandmother in Minori and my mother decided to come with me. This was to be the first reunion with my grandmother since she left England immediately before the start of the Second World War in 1939 – eleven years since I last saw her, though I never did tell her what had happened to me during that time.

I felt closer to my mother on that holiday than at any other time in my life. We travelled across the Channel and caught a train to Rome where we visited the Vatican, wherein I didn't make the sign of the cross, which disappointed my mother. After visiting the Coliseum, St Peter's Basilica and the Sistine Chapel we caught another train to Salerno and a bus to Minori. It was lovely seeing my Nanny again. Though less nimble, she had retained her vitality and sense of humour but still found it hard to get her head around the English language. She was now living in a fairly spartan one bedroomed apartment in an old fortress. It had half-metre thick walls with windows and a small balcony looking out to sea. Outside was a stone staircase leading to a roof area and, being September, Nanny had spread out many halved tomatoes to dry in the sun. She used the sun-dried tomatoes in her mouth-watering dishes that she cooked but she also bartered any surplus for groceries and other essentials. I had a feeling of déjà vu to the smells in the cafés, the tobacconists' shops and the herb and vegetable shops. I had a feeling I had come home.

I did notice the absence of bird-life and Nanny explained to me that many people caught them in nets and cooked them. Luckily, we never experienced this culinary delight. The town seemed austere with no electricity in many of the shops. Nanny seemed happy enough but I could not understand why she lived in such a place when she owned a twenty-two roomed villa in Sorrento which was rented out as apartments, not that I ever visited the house. Years later I was given to understand that the rentals were set at a very low rate and could not be increased unless, or until, someone moved out. This was her only means of financial support and none of her tenants moved.

John's Grandmother Trofimena and relative, possibly Diana, with kittens. Cat sitting named by John as 'Belvedere'. Minori 1950s.

I went swimming each day and took long walks, usually alone, along narrow passageways, past beautiful terraced gardens ablaze with bougainvillaea, lemon trees and hanging vines, till I reached the lovely villas of Ravello overlooking the bay of Amalfi. Local people and Italian relatives were very hospitable. We were even invited to lunch in Amalfi where I fell in love with one of the

family's beautiful daughters called Tetina Ciano. I was besotted, and eventually proposed. Thereafter, we were escorted wherever we went, as is the custom. Our relationship didn't go further than that. After I left to join the Army she wrote to me for a long time. I had her letters translated by the Army Chaplain, but eventually our friendship petered out.

My mother did come with me to Pompeii and we visited the markets in Salerno. I loved Positano, Amalfi, Ravello and Naples and visited the run-down cinema in Maiori, the village east of Minori. It seemed strange to see old American films dubbed with 'posh' Italian accents. I had the best holiday I have ever had in my life because of the memories and smells of my youth.

Two days after my return from the holiday in Minori I reported for Military Service at Aldershot. This was the time when I separated almost completely from my mother, and though I saw her a few times over the years, I never again stayed under the same roof with her. She had little interest in continuing our association. When on leave from the Army I used to stay with my Auntie Emily in Onslow Road, Southampton, and once I had an extended leave in Minori with my grandmother.

My intention was to train in the Army as a Dental Technician but by the time I joined they had sufficient numbers, so I was trained to be a Dentist's Clerk and later a Chair-side Assistant rather like a Dental Nurse. We didn't do any rifle training because we were considered 'non-combatants' but we did marching, which we called 'square bashing', at which I wasn't particularly good. I was sent to Portsmouth for a year, then overseas to several different towns in Germany. One place was Lippstadt where I met a young German lady called Charlotte Simone. We almost got to the point of getting married though we lost contact when I was returned to England but it did mean at the time that I was involved in the German culture, which I loved.

John's enlistment in the Army Dental Corps, Aldershot, Hampshire.

closeness. I was more interested in being driven around the twisting Amalfi coast road on the back of a scooter driven by one of my young relatives. This was to be the last time I saw my grandmother. I never saw her again, and she died ten years later. I remember she used to say to me "Piu conosco gli uomini, piu amo le bestie". (The more I learn about people, the more I love the animals!)

During this Leave I received a telegram requesting me to report urgently for duty. As I hadn't been asked to sign for it, I pretended I hadn't received it. When I did eventually get back to Germany I learnt I had been given a 'rank' and was to have been sent to Bermuda. Because I hadn't returned as instructed, I was transferred to Aldershot, the posting was cancelled and I was sent to an Army Training Camp at Gatwick. From there I was sent to York to join the King's Own Yorkshire

Whilst in Germany I decided to accumulate my Leave to one month and spent the whole time with my grandmother in Minori. With my Army cigarette allowance I was able to buy twenty cigarettes for one shilling. Since I no longer smoked, I had accumulated around fifty thousand cigarettes which I took in a suitcase to Minori to sell. Luckily, when Italian Customs Officers boarded my train they didn't bother to search my case. As soon as I said I was English they just said that was 'OK' and went on their way. That was a great relief. I also bought a huge amount of Army 'French letters' to sell but, of course, Italy is a Catholic country so I had to throw them away! I sold all the cigarettes though, and that helped to pay for my vacation.

It was very nice to be with my grandmother, though at twenty-one and with so many years apart from her, I did not feel the same

John on leave.

Light Infantry where we had to march at the double! The Dental Centre was fine though and I made a lot of friends amongst the cooks – I ate well! At York I applied to train as a Dental Hygienist. The Officer who interviewed me probably thought I hadn't had a suitable education and instead I was posted to Dental Army Stores at a disused RAF airfield at Pocklington. The stores, which contained dental and medical equipment, were in a real mess and sorting out the contents was a dangerous task. I took my Christmas Leave at New Year because I loved to be with the Scots at Hogmanay.

Pocklington was my last posting. I had been in the Army from 1949 to 1953 and had enjoyed the life but didn't wish to sign up again, especially as the pay was very low. I needed a change and a new challenge. I left the Army and went to live temporarily with my Auntie Emily, Pete Ashton and Bruce. Auntie Emily's unofficially adopted son was now eight years old. I got a job via the Labour Exchange as a trainee technician in a laboratory at Esso Oil Refinery, Fawley, just outside Southampton. There was a good wage with this job – in fact, I had never had so much money. I eventually lived in their hostel for single people which was close to the site gates. I stayed in that job for a couple of years.

In those days you could move from job to job very easily and I got a job in the car industry in Swindon, welding car doors. By then I had bought my first car and I shared the car journey with other workers on Mondays, stayed in Swindon mid-week, and we all came back together on Fridays. However, the job didn't suit me because I was forced to join the Union. I soon discovered there was a strike every Monday for no reason except that the workers wanted to go to the pub until two o'clock, after which time they'd go back to work! Thereafter, I stayed in a job for six months working as a lorry driver for a stonemason's company in Southampton. I found it interesting to watch the skilled masons doing their work.

At the time, I rented a room in the house of my cousin, Mena Peden, in Bitterne. It was so nice to be back with my cousin. I liked doing artistic hobbies, including cooking and gardening, and I did some for Mena. I also started to collect special coins.

After I left the stonemason's company, I got a job in a chemical industry with Union Carbide at Hythe, just outside Southampton. This company didn't have a very good safety record and risks were taken that would not be allowed today. It was just pure luck that I survived one or two incidents involving the handling of 100% hydrogen peroxide and toxic powders. Whilst I was working at Union Carbide I was able to get a mortgage with the Oddfellows Society and I bought a little two-up, two-down cottage with a bit of surrounding land in Holbury. I raised six hundred pounds in mortgage, plus three hundred pounds in a loan from the Westminster Bank, making the nine hundred pounds it cost. I was now on the housing ladder and considered this to be my first proper home. I felt proud.

CHAPTER FIVE
MARRIED LIFE

MY COUSIN MENA WAS working at the Telephone Exchange in Southampton and she contacted me to ask if I would like to take on some extra work painting the outside of a bungalow in Totton belonging to a colleague of hers. The owner of the bungalow was a lady called Helen Barn. She was to become my wife and I never did get paid for the painting! Helen was fifteen years older than me and a divorcee, but we were attracted to one another and felt happy together. We got on so well that I asked her to marry me. On the 30th September 1961 I married Helen at the Church of Scotland in Brunswick Place, Southampton. Since Helen was Scottish we drove to Scotland for our honeymoon in a car that used more oil than petrol!

John and Helen in Southampton, 1962.

A few years later I discovered there were jobs for experienced operators on offer at Gulf Oil Petro-chemical plant at Milford Haven, South Wales. A colleague of mine and I decided to apply and since we both got jobs we were able to share a furniture removals lorry. Helen and I bought a beautiful house suitable for renovation. It was right on the beach at Llanstadwell and looked out onto the Haven. We lived there for twelve years from 1968 until 1980 and this was probably the happiest time of our marriage as we were then very much a couple. We bought a second-hand little speed boat and we had great fun rushing out to the Heads or fishing. Helen wasn't particularly keen on the boat so I mostly went sailing on my own or took friends. I had a few worrying times with the boat on the shingle and the mud but I really enjoyed the pastime. With other volunteers, I took handicapped children to the swimming baths, and I also took up yoga.

The work at the oil refinery was on the petro-chemical side where we produced cyclohexane and raphinate which is the base for petrol. The job had its safety risks but lessons had been learnt by the Flixborough disaster in Lincolnshire in 1974 when an explosion wrecked the whole chemical plant killing twenty-eight and injuring many others. At the time we supplied Flixborough with cyclohexane.

After twelve years in the job I began to get itchy feet and wanted to see other places so I got a job overseas working for Pullman-Kellogg in Algeria. Helen didn't mind. She and I were two of a kind in that we both liked change. We sold our house in Milford Haven and moved to Anstruther in Fife, Scotland.

My job in Algeria was near Skikda, previously called Philippeville, which is on the north coast. I was working on a cryogenic plant which was mining gas, super-cooling it and separating out its water content. We weren't paid danger money but our contracts were

An Algerian scene.

good, though the jobs were absolutely awful. After a couple of weeks I had some great luck because I was offered a job on the water treatment plant within the same camp. The water was pumped from a well that the French had used prior to the Algerian War of Independence in the 1950s which didn't end until 1962. My job was to properly chlorinate and keep the water flowing so as to supply the whole camp. I worked a twelve hour day but as the job didn't really take that long I made myself look busy for fear of being told to work in the actual plant as well. I got on well with everybody, including the Algerians, mostly because I was in charge of the water supply. I had a lucky escape from certain death one time when an Algerian child was killed by a hit-and-run driver. The Algerians were looking for 'an eye for an eye',

John drinking water he purified, Pullman-Kellog Camp, Skikda (Phillipville), Algeria, 1982.

and they didn't care who it was. Driving back to the camp one day a hoard of local people surrounded my vehicle and pulled me out. At the time I didn't know what it was all about but as luck would have it an Algerian recognised me as the man who provided free water to them all and they soon agreed that I should be allowed to go on my way.

I worked a four month stretch, and then had two weeks leave. I sometimes chose to fly home via Geneva where I could buy Algerian dinars which I sold at a profit to the other workers when I returned to Algeria. That was the one and only time I ventured into that sort of activity. Algerians were willing to sell dinars to us but they were often arrested for having pounds sterling in their possession and then they would spill the beans about who bought their dinars which were an illegal currency at the time.

I wrote to Helen almost every day and she kept all those letters which are now stored in the loft. The air flight home was paid by Pullman-Kellogg and Helen and I spent some lovely holidays together. We even bought a

flat for £7,000 in Majorca. Later on we bought the flat next to it and converted the two into one larger apartment with two bedrooms and two bathrooms. For seventeen years we enjoyed holidays there and when we weren't there our friends used it, though we never rented it out.

After a couple of years the Algerians terminated their contract with Pullman-Kellogg which meant the whole camp had to be disbanded. It was rumoured that Pullman-Kellogg had been charging the Algerians ten percent over the purchase price of anything they sold to them. However, the Algerians asked me to stay on for four or five months to train an Algerian to run the water system. I said I would, so long as my wife could join me for the last few weeks. They reluctantly agreed and Helen found the visit really enjoyable and interesting. I had to work extremely hard training the Algerian in how not to let things drift. Just before Helen and I left we ensured we spent all our redundant dinars. We went to a market near a marble quarry and bought marble lamps, table cigarette lighters,

John in Madinat al Jubail near Dubai, with Arab colleagues.

138

ornaments and vases. We also upgraded our flight to Business Class, paying in dinars. When we got home to Scotland we had a big disappointment, for after paying the freight charges, insurance and import duty, which together with the purchase price amounted to hundreds of pounds, we discovered that the marble objects were of such low quality that we could not use, sell nor give them away! I later learnt that the best Algerian marble was directly exported, leaving the poorer quality for local customers, such as we were at the time.

On returning to our lovely house at Melville Terrace, Anstruther I was unemployed for a while so I offered my services to the Scottish Fisheries Museum where Helen too did voluntary work. The Queen and Prince Phillip visited the Museum whilst we were there and we were involved in a hive of activity prior to their visit. However, I needed to get work so we sold up and moved back to Southampton where we bought a very nice semi-detached house in Lansdowne Road, Regent's Park. I soon got a job working for a French Consortium on a water transmission pipeline between Dhahran and Riyadh in Saudi Arabia though the job only lasted for six months. Thereafter, I worked near Madinat al Jubail near Dubai producing crude industrial ethanol. The strict Saudi laws prohibited the production of pure ethanol. Whilst working there I was lucky to escape a terrorist attack on one of the huge oil tanks. Luckily for me the explosion happened in the evening and I had been working the day shift.

I worked for three months at a time, then had two weeks leave. Helen and I used to travel to France for some of our vacations and we bought a derelict house in Ballon, Charante Maritime. Part of the house was built in 1712. It was quite a big venture but it had a water supply and I looked forward to the challenge of undertaking the renovation. The area was very tranquil and the French people were very nice. Nevertheless, after about three years we had to admit defeat through cost and time and we sold it to a young French couple who fell in love with it.

John and Helen at their holiday home, Ballon, Charante Maritime, France, 1986.

John with his cousin Elise's daughter, Sophie Edwards. A French playmate on the right. At John's holiday home in France.

I then got a job with BP at Wytch Farm near Poole in Dorset so we 'upped sticks' yet again and bought a bungalow in Poole. Again we renovated this and added two garages and a conservatory. However, my job contract came to an end after a couple of years and in any event, I got a much better job working as a contractor for British Gas on an off-shore platform in Morecambe Bay where I stayed for the last ten years of my working life. We found a suitable, well-built detached house in a place called Bare. The job was dangerous but we were well-trained. We were flown by helicopter to the rig which was twelve miles off-shore. The stringency of the safety precautions was unbelievable. My job involved the process of making the gas as water-free as possible. I stayed on the rig working for two weeks at a stretch, then had two weeks' leave. This job lasted until my retirement in 1998, by which time I had added quite a bit to my pension.

It was whilst we were living in Morecambe that my mother and Auntie Emily came to stay for a holiday but they didn't stay for long. Things did not go well because Helen could not take to my mother and it seemed my mother resented someone who was close in age to herself being married to her son. Helen objected very strongly to me having contact with anyone from the Donnarumma family so I kept the peace, though I some-times made a surreptitious call from a street telephone box or met with my aunts or cousins en route to France to renovate our house there. My mother lived for many years with a man called Bill Smith who was very good to her and they eventually married for reasons of convenience though they never had children. I never spoke to my mother, my family, my wife, nor anyone, about the abuse I experienced at the hands of the Sisters of Nazareth. It was too painful to look back and I had to get on with my life.

CHAPTER SIX
RETIREMENT

WHILST WE WERE LIVING in Morecambe we bought a cottage in Strathmiglow in Fife which we used as a holiday retreat. On my retirement we were able to sell this and together with the capital from the sale of our house in Morecambe, we were able to buy the four-bedroomed bungalow here in Gauldry, Fife. Helen was back on her home ground with her relatives around her and I was able to enjoy the wonderful landscape and area.

There was never an occasion in our married life when Helen was despondent or unhappy about moving. She too looked forward to the adventure and expectancy of something new – new friends, new places, new experiences. Helen eventually became disabled and was confined to a wheelchair. I cared for her until she died in February 2010 aged ninety-two. Helen and I had been very much a couple when we were younger but as the years went by we had drifted apart a bit, which wasn't anything unusual. We had a good marriage which lasted almost fifty years.

Looking back, there were a lot of times when I was living in the orphanage and being badly treated when I felt neglected, hurt, disliked or hated, but nature seemed to mend things. I managed to get over sad events as part of nature's course and to get on with life.

John and Helen at Rannoch Moor station café during their retirement, 2002.

I've never felt despondent. As a small boy I never thought of my mother because I didn't know I had one, and from the age of five I didn't know my grandmother. Perhaps this was because 'mother nature' was helping me to feel excited about experiencing something new and I was concentrating on that. It's nice to talk on the telephone to my old pals from Wardour, Brian Osborne, Larry Barnett or John Savage. Amongst other things, we feel we can now talk freely about the abuse we suffered. It feels good for things to be in the open. Not that some of us can be bothered now, but an apology from the Roman Catholic Church would subdue my feelings of injustice.

My retirement is filled with activities. I do voluntary driving for the Royal Voluntary Service as well as visiting isolated older or blind people. I love designing my garden, cooking, do-it-yourself, yoga and writing poetry. I read, watch television programmes and am interested in many aspects of life.

John in his back garden, Gauldry, Fife, 2011.

I am very happy living alone. I feel more contented now than I've ever felt before because I've achieved everything I want or could need – a lovely bungalow and a good standard of living. I can go where I please, and do what I please, though at the age of eighty-one I don't feel like travelling too far from this area. Helen's nieces and nephews live close-by and visit me, and since my wife's death I have become reunited with some of my Donnarumma cousins. We keep in constant touch on the telephone. Mena has visited once, and Elise Donnarumma Edwards, her daughter Sophie Hardy and family visit me a couple of times a year. I consider I have a good life now.

Ode to Hilda Clow, the Yoga Teacher by John Donnarumma Richardson.

*Guiding the class through yoga tuition
In mode of jocund agility,
From inverted posture to cobra position
Adhered to a cache of abilities
To keep us all in prime condition,
Few can match your expertise!*

*Willpower and dedication, that's the need,
With determination to succeed!
Stretch and balance, touch the toes,
See the weight, how quick it goes!
Stretch and balance, breath control,
That's the way to reach the goal!*

*In yoga practice you are a perfectionist,
Ranking you a prodigious artist!
You set an example, none can dismiss!
Not a single session ever missed,
Not even when you broke your wrist!*

*This little ode to you we give
With love and appreciation,
For you are impressive and progressive
And to us all an inspiration!
Shanti! Shanti! Shanti! ('Peace')*

John Donnarumma Richardson in his kilt before attending a special dinner, 2012. Note the photo of Minori on the wall. John's grandmother's apartment in the tallest building looked out to sea.

ACKNOWLEDGMENTS

I should like to thank, most profusely, the family of Mr Edward Freestone, notably his eldest daughter, Mrs Kim Cox; Mrs Erika Brooke, nee Jennova, and Mr John (Donnarumma) Richardson. Thank you for trusting me with your life stories. I hope I have done them justice. Thank you also to Mrs Phyllis McGregor of Auchterarder, Scotland for giving me some insight into the life of Mr Norman Drummond. Your patience and all your contributions have been immense. Ultimately, my recordings will be placed in the Sound Archives of the British Library or Imperial War Museum, where they will be preserved and listened to by future generations.

The journey of producing this book has been an all-absorbing education and privilege. I have met many friendly, helpful people along my route whom I thank hereunder according to 'Section' order of the book.

Dr George Rawson, Art Historian, Glasgow. Maggie Wilson, National Museums Scotland, Edinburgh. Michelle Kay and Volunteers, the Glasgow School of Art. Mrs Joy Freestone and children, Kim, Neil, Sharon and Simon. Paul and Sheila Dainton of Leigh, Lancashire. Helli and Dieter Mansius of Oberwern, Schweinfurt, Bavaria. Dr Susan Calvert, Southampton. Elise Edwards (nee Donnarumma), Mena Miguel, Anthony and Barbara Donnarumma, Brian and Pat Osborne, John Savage, all of Hampshire. Larry Barnett of California, USA. Brian and Barbara Doherty of Woolwich, London. Barry Williamson of Bristol.

The Archive staff of the following organisations: The British Red Cross, London. The International Committee of the Red Cross and Red Crescent Movement, Geneva. The Bournemouth Library and History Centre. Bournemouth Cemeteries Department. The Dorset History Centre, Dorchester. Southampton Special Collections and Archives. Hampshire Record Office, Winchester. Bridport Museum. The Quaker Museum, London. Wiltshire and Swindon History Centre, Chippenham. Coalbrookdale Museum, Ironbridge. Mr Norbert Wittl, Public Relations Officer, Joint Multinational Training Command, Hohenfels, Bavaria. The Polish Army Office, Torun. The National Archives at Kew. The Anglo-Italian Family History Society, St Peter's Italian Church, Holborn, London. The Imperial War Museum, London. The Oral History Society. South Coast Echo Newspapers. Signore Antonio Pappalardo, L'Ufficiale dello Stato Civile, Minori, Italy.

My appreciation goes to my Book Designer, Matt Swann for his creative work and great patience. Thank you also to the Staff of Hobbs the Printers and to David Hobbs for his generous support of the Red Cross. A special thank you to Mr John (Donnarumma) Richardson for his generous support of the Red Cross.

Family photographs have been provided by the Freestone, Brooke, Jennova, Richardson, MacGregor and Donnarumma families. The original aerial photograph of Wardour Castle is in the possession of Major General Patrick Fagan. All other photograph credits appear in the text. Every effort has been made to trace copyright holders. Apologies in advance if an oversight has occurred.

Thank you to my son, Alastair, for casting a critical eye over my life story of Arthur Vincent Aston-Nicholas, and to both my sons, Alastair and Julian, over my Prologue on Henry Dunant. Thank you to my sister, Jeanne Simkin, for proof-reading the manuscript and for her generous support of the Red Cross. Last, but not least, a special thank you to my husband, Andrew, for his generous support of the Red Cross, and for his assistance with the execution of cameras, scanners and computers. He also drove with me through Europe in pursuit of my research, and at times sat alongside me, camera at the ready, in dark and dusty archives.

BIBLIOGRAPHY

Prologue

Beecher Stowe, Harriet. (1852) "Uncle Tom's Cabin".

Bennett, Angela. (2005) "The Geneva Convention – the Hidden Origins of the Red Cross". Sutton Publishing Ltd. Stroud.

Dunant, Jean-Henri. (1862) "Un Souvenir de Solferino" – A Memory of Solferino. SG Frick, Geneva.

Gumpert, Martin. (1938) "Dunant - The Story of the Red Cross". New York, Oxford University Press.

Hart, Ellen. (1953) "Man Born to Live – Life and Work of Henry Dunant, Founder of the International Red Cross". Gollanz, London.

International Committee of the Red Cross, Geneva, Switzerland. "A Memory of Solferino", "The Origins of the Red Cross", "The Story of an Idea", "The ICRC – Its Mission and Work", "The Fundamental Principles of the Red Cross and Red Crescent", "ICRC Strategy 2015-2018", "Basic Rules of the Geneva Conventions and Their Additional Protocols". www.icrc.org

Moorehead, Caroline. (1998) "Dunant's Dream – War, Switzerland and the History of the Red Cross". Harper Collins, London.

Section One

Boynton, Helen and Dickens, Keith. (2006) "Leicester and its Suburbs in the 1920s and '30s". Helen Boynton, Leicester.

Capa, Robert. (1947) "Slightly Out of Focus. The Legendary Photojournalist's Illustrated Memoir of World War II". Henry Holt & Co.Inc. 1999 Random House. Inc.

Crawley, Aidan. (2009) "Escape from Germany – True Stories of POW Escapes in WWII". Introduction by Graham Pitchfork. The National Archives UK.

Dainton, Paul. (2009) "Lance-Corporal Thomas Dainton of the Royal Army Service Corps, 1939-1945". Self-published. Leigh, Lancashire.

Evans, AA and Gibbons, David. (2008) "The Compact Timeline of World War II". Worth Press Ltd. Herts UK.

Ferguson, Niall. (2006) "The War of the World. Twentieth Century Conflict and the Descent of the West". Penguin Group.

Foot, MRD & Langley, JM. (1979) "MI9 - Escape and Evasion 1939-1945". Book Club Associates by arrangement with Bodley Head.

Gillies, Midge. (2011) "The Barbed-Wire University. The Real Lives of Prisoners of War in the Second World War". Aurum Press Ltd. London.

Greasley, Horace. (2013) "Do the Birds Still Sing in Hell". John Blake Publishing Ltd. London.

Hastings, Max. (2011) "All Hell Let Loose. The World at War 1939–1945". Harper Press. London.

McKibbin, M.N. (1947) "Barbed Wire – Memories of Stalag 383". Illustrated by A.G. Dallimore. Staples Press Ltd. Cavendish Place and Great Titchfield Street, London, New York and Toronto.

Oral History Team, Southampton. (1989) "Woolston Before the Bridge". Sheila Jemima, Christine Tanner, Donald Hyslop. Southampton Local Studies Section.

Richardson, Matthew. (2010) "Tigers at Dunkirk. The Leicestershire Regiment and the Fall of France". Pen & Sword Military Imprint, Barnsley, S.Yorks.

Rollings, Charles. (2003) "Wire and Walls. RAF Prisoners of War in Itzehoe, Spangenberg and Thorn 1939-1942". Ian Allan Publishing, Surrey.

Rollings, Charles. (2008) "Prisoner of War. Voices from Behind the Wire in the Second World War". Ebury Publishing, Random House Group.

Say, Rosemary and Holland, Noel. (2011) "Rosie's War. An Englishwoman's Escape from Occupied France". Michael O'Mara Books Ltd. London.

Shirer, William L. (1960) "The Rise and Fall of the Third Reich". Secker & Warburg Ltd. 1975 Pan Books, London.

Stourton, Edward. (2013) "Cruel Crossing. Escaping Hitler Across the Pyrenees". Doubleday imprint of Transworld Publishers.

Wynne Mason, W. (1954) "Prisoners of War – Official History of New Zealand in the Second World War 1939-1945". War History Branch, Dept of Internal Affairs, Wellington, New Zealand.

Section Two

Anonymous. (2006) "A Woman in Berlin". Introduction by Anthony Beevor. Virago Press. First published 1954 by Harcourt Brace Jonavich, New York.

Edgington, M.A. (1994) "Bournemouth and the Second World War 1939-1945". Bournemouth Local Studies Publications, Dorset.

Ferguson, Hugh. (1995) "Glasgow School of Art. The History". The Foulis Press of Glasgow School of Art.

Gillman, Peter and Leni. (1980) "Collar the Lot. How Britain Interned and Expelled Its Wartime Refugees". Quartet Books Ltd, London.

Hirschfeld, Gerhard. Ed. (1984) "Exile in Great Britain – Refugees from Hitler's Germany". Berg Publishers Ltd. Warwickshire.

Judt, Tony. (2010) "Postwar. A History of Europe Since 1945". Vintage Books, London.

Kochan, Miriam. (1980) "Prisoners of England". The MacMillan Press Ltd. London and Basingstoke.

Lafitte, F. (1940). "The Internment of Aliens". Penguin Books Ltd. Harmondsworth, England and New York.

Lowe, Keith. (2012) "Savage Continent. Europe in the Aftermath of the World War II". Penguin Viking.

Macdonald, Stuart. (1970) "The History and Philosophy of Art Education". University of London Press Ltd.

McKenzie, Roy. Ed. (2009) "The Flower and the Green Leaf. Glasgow School of Art in the Time of Charles Rennie Mackintosh". Glasgow School of Art.

Rawson, George. (1996) "Fra H Newbery, Artist and Art Educationist 1855–1946". The Foulis Press of Glasgow School of Art.

Rawson, George. (2008) "Fra H Newbery – A Dorset Artist". Produced through "Fra H Newbery – A Dorset Trail". Bridport Heritage Forum, Dorset.

Schneider, Bronka. (1998) "Exile: A Memoir of 1939". The Ohio State University, USA.

Section Three

Boyne, John. (2014) "A History of Loneliness". Doubleday, an imprint of Transworld Publishers.

Colpi, Terri (1991) "The Italian Factor – The Italian Community in Great Britain". Mainstream Publishing.

Colpi, Terri. (1991) "A Visual History of the Italian Community in Great Britain". Mainstream Publishing.

Diamand, Dr Salim. (1987) "Dottore! – Internment in Italy 1940-1945". Mosaic Press, USA and London.

Doherty, Brian. (2006) "Ex-Home Boy's Memoirs, Fahan Termonbacca and Nazareth House 1892-1982. Self-published, London. ISBN 0-9548435-0-9.

Ford, Percy. (1931) "Work and Wealth in a Modern Port – An Economic Survey of Southampton". George Allen and Unwin Ltd. D.Phil Thesis, University of London.

Giblin, Mary Josephine. (1927) "Stories of Nazareth House". Sands & Co, London, Edinburgh and Glasgow.

Gadd, Eric Wyeth. (1988) "Southampton Through this Century". Paul Cave Publications Ltd.

Gadd, Eric Wyeth. (1979) "Southampton in the Twenties". Paul Cave Publications Ltd.

Gallaher, Tony. (1995) "Southampton's Inns and Taverns". Poulner Publishing Ltd. Ringwood, Hampshire.

Hodgson, Maie. (1992) "Child of the Ditches". Typeset and printed by Fleetwood Print, Southampton.

Humphreys, Margaret. (1994) "Empty Cradles - One Woman's Fight to Uncover Britain's Most Shameful Secret". Transworld Publishers Ltd, London, Sydney, Auckland.

Jemima, Sheila. Ed. (1991) "Chapel and Northam – An Oral History of Southampton's Dockland Communities 1900-1945". Southampton City Council.

Sandell, Elsie M. (1953) "Southampton Cavalcade". G.F. Wilson & Co Ltd. Southampton.

Sandell, Elsie M. (1958) "Southampton Panorama". G.F. Wilson & Co Ltd. Southampton.

Sponza, Lucio. (1988) "Italian Immigrants in Nineteenth Century Britain: Realities and Images". Leicester University Press.

Sponza, Lucio. (2000) "Divided Loyalties – Italians in Britain During the Second World War". Peter Lang AG European Academic Publishers, Bern.

Tanner, Christine P. (2011) "Carlo's Ice Cream Parlour and Tea Rooms – Generational Oral History of an Anglo-Italian Family". CPT Oral History, Wiltshire. www.cptoralhistory.blogspot.com   cptoralhistory@gmail.com

Tanner, Christine P. (1993) "Coming to Terms with the Past – The Life Review and Its Applications in Social Work and Probation Practice". Unpublished MSc Dissertation, Southampton University.

Ugolini, Wendy. (2011) "Experiencing War as the 'Enemy Other' – Italian Scottish Experience in World War II". Manchester University Press.

Williamson, Barry. (2011) "The Arundells of Wardour – from Cornwall to Colditz". Hobnob Press, East Knoyle, Salisbury, Wiltshire.

www.ancestry.co.uk www.findmypast.co.uk   www.nationalarchives.gov.uk
www.wikipedia.org   www.scotlandspeople.gov.uk www.familysearch.org